ARKANA

ZEN AND US

Acclaimed throughout Europe as the leading reconciler of Oriental and Western thought, Karlfried Graf Dürckheim had an astounding life. Born into the Bavarian nobility, he survived four years at the front in World War I and was saved at the last minute from a Spartacist firing squad during the abortive Bavarian Revolution of 1919. He later gave up his inheritance to undergo spiritual training as a psychologist and philosopher. Influenced by his association with Klee, Kandinsky, and Mies van der Rohe, his initiation into an esoteric group in Munich, and his studies with Heidegger, D. T. Suzuki, and others, he spent the Nazi years in Japan and went on to found the world-famous Center for Initiatory Psychotherapy in the Black Forest after World War II. His best-known works in English to date are *Hara: The Vital Centre of Man* and *The Way of Transformation: Daily Life as Spiritual Exercise*. His most recently translated work is *Absolute Living*.

OTHER BOOKS BY
KARLFRIED GRAF DÜRCKHEIM IN ENGLISH

The Way of Transformation: Daily Life as Spiritual Exercise

Hara: The Vital Centre of Man

The Grace of Zen: Zen Texts for Meditation
(with others)

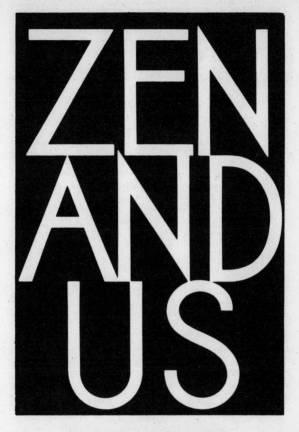

ZEN AND US

KARLFRIED GRAF DÜRCKHEIM

Translated from the German by Vincent Nash

ARKANA

ARKANA
Published by the Penguin Group
Viking Penguin, a division of Penguin Books USA Inc.,
375 Hudson Street, New York, New York 10014, U.S.A.
Penguin Books Ltd, 27 Wrights Lane, London W8 5TZ, England
Penguin Books Australia Ltd, Ringwood, Victoria, Australia
Penguin Books Canada Ltd, 10 Alcorn Avenue, Suite 300,
Toronto, Ontario, Canada M4V 3B2
Penguin Books (N.Z.) Ltd, 182–190 Wairau Road,
Auckland 10, New Zealand

Penguin Books Ltd, Registered Offices:
Harmondsworth, Middlesex, England

First published in the United States of America by E. P. Dutton 1987
Published simultaneously in Canada by Fitzhenry and Whiteside, Limited, Toronto
Published in Arkana 1991

1 3 5 7 9 10 8 6 4 2

Originally published in West Germany under the title *Zen und Wir*.

ISBN 0 14 01.9346 4

Printed in the United States of America
Designed by Michele Aldin

For Maria Hippius

Editor's Note

Quotations from Buddhist texts, as for example the section from the *Shin Jin Mei* on page 63 and the hymn attributed to Buddha on page 67, have been translated from the author's German in an effort to preserve a unity of tone and the author's interpretative intent. There exist, however, some very notable translations of these same texts by such figures as D. T. Suzuki, R. H. Blythe, and others.

Contents

Preface

What was said in the first German edition of this book regarding the significance of Zen for people in the West has proved true. The waves of Zen have beaten powerfully in upon the Western mind since then. But taking up Zen in the West can mean two things: becoming a Buddhist or opening oneself to the general, human significance of Zen's message. The second aspect is the only one that concerns me here. I know it is sometimes thought that Zen cannot be divorced from its Buddhist origins, and that Zen is Buddhism or nothing. This may be true for the theorist who, having no personal experience of the doctrine that true nature (Buddha-nature) is present in all of us, sees Zen as a purely Eastern vision of the human condition, or knows it only from books or as a tourist. Anyone, however, who is not deaf to the Absolute or who has spent some time on one of the Zen exercises—zazen, for example—soon finds that Zen is concerned with the basis of all genuine religious feeling, and indeed of all human growth and maturity. Zen enables us to do two things: first, to become one with our "true nature," in which the Absolute is present within us; and, second, to fulfill our human destiny by transforming ourselves and becoming a transparent medium, so that the Absolute within us can shine through. Zazen—seated meditation, in which meditation is not "contemplation," but a way of change—is a sober, stern, and rigorous exercise. It provides a healthy antidote to the ecstasy-seeking so popular today, and its emphasis on physical discipline brings it close both to the Western concern with personal form and the Christian conception of spirit becoming flesh. Its truth is universal and rooted in experience, and the encounter with it will help us to rediscover that truth and that experience in our own tradition—and revitalize our own spiritual life.

Starting Points

What Has Zen Got to Do with Us in the West?

What has Zen got to do with us in the West? Everyone, everywhere, is talking about Zen. Everything published on Zen at once finds eager readers. Where does this strange attraction come from? Is it a passing fashion? Is it the lure of the exotic? Is it a way out of our own problems and into another, faraway world? All of this may be partly true—but the fascination really comes from something else.

People today are aware that there is something basically wrong with current social values. Deep down, they know that the ways of thinking and acting that are supposed to enable them to cope with "outside" life are really undermining their own inner life—and they suffer increasingly from this knowledge. With no beliefs left to sustain them, they run from themselves, from this growing inner emptiness, and seek ref-

3

uge in outside distractions. They lose contact with themselves, and their inner breathing falters. Feelings of guilt and fear take over. Bewildered and rudderless, they look around desperately for a way out. If, at this point, they happen on a text by one of the Zen masters, something deeper speaks to them immediately. They seem to breathe a new freedom. They feel as if a spring breeze had suddenly melted the icebound crust of their existence, as if a new liberty were being promised and a hidden life called into being. This is what makes Zen, in all its forms, attractive: it promises to free our real life, our real being, from the falsehoods and confusion that stifle it.

Zen speaks with vital force, and whenever it speaks, it breaks through the crust of what is and shows that it can become something else. It smashes through the tidy ideas, concepts, and images that prop us up and help to keep us going, but also shut us off from the real life within us—a life that expresses itself in a never-ending process of renewal. Zen touches the reality within us—Life, which transforms, redeems, and creates without ceasing, which is always on the way to becoming something else and which cannot be pinned down to any fixed form. Zen throws the door wide and points the way into the open. This is why it shakes the orderly citizen in all of us, with our fondness for well-worn daily routines; why it threatens the guardians of accepted values; why it enrages all those who rely on "systems" to keep their little worlds running smoothly; why it is also deeply disturbing for all of us who feel that nothing is "real" unless we can understand it rationally. Zen offers us something that lies wholly beyond that kind of understanding. But this is precisely what makes it so attractive and so promising for all of us who are sick of leading lives deadened by indolence, set ideas, and easy comfort, and who are looking for new horizons, thirsting for real life—real life that catches fire only when we make the leap from the safe and relative into the perilous and absolute.

The Light from the East?

Zen promises us something radically new—but why should this come from the East? Surely the mysterious spring flows in the West as well? It does indeed, but only in secret—hidden or discredited by the thrust of the Western mentality's development. In the East, everyone has always known where to find it, and its waters were guided long ago into a complex system of canals that kept them flowing. But is the East still what it was? Surely westernization has left it with nothing of its own to tell us? This is a question that people are constantly asking today. But just as the significance of ancient Greek culture for us in the West is in no way diminished by what may have happened to the Greeks in the meantime, so the significance of the Oriental spirit and its achievements is in no way affected by the political, economic, or even intellectual development of the peoples of Japan, China, and India. This development often seems to threaten the surviving manifestations of the ancient Oriental outlook—but it may in fact be bringing the spirit of the East home to us fully for the first time. This becomes clearer if we realize that the avidity with which the peoples of the East are seizing on Western ideas and life-styles reflects not only the need for Western products and technology as keys to survival and power, but also the deeper need to develop, at long last, a side of the human spirit that they have so far neglected and that human beings need in order to be complete: the rational side, which helps us to explain the world about us and cope with it in practice.

Conversely, the more we are led by an obscure attraction to explore the manifestations of the ancient Oriental mind, the clearer it can and should become that the tension we feel between the Eastern and the Western mentalities ultimately has nothing to do with cultural differences, but expresses a basic human dilemma. Depth psychology has shown that a man cannot be a complete human being, and thus a complete man, unless he recognizes the feminine side of his nature, takes it seriously, and tries to develop it. In the same

5

way, we Westerners cannot be complete human beings and fulfill our destinies as complete Westerners unless we recognize and develop something that at first seems Oriental, but is actually waiting in every one of us to be noticed and acknowledged.

In a specifically Eastern form, the Eastern spirit embodies human qualities and possibilities that the Western mentality has obscured and prevented from developing properly, even though human beings are incomplete without them. To this extent, the experience and wisdom of Buddhism, and particularly of Zen, are not simply Eastern, but of universal human significance—indeed of very special significance in an age that has given us such frightening proofs of the dangers of developing our capabilities in one direction only.

What Zen Is Essentially About

Zen is essentially about rebirth from the experience of Being.

Zen teaches us to discover the transcendental core of our own selves in an immediate and practical sense, to "taste" divine Being in the here-and-now. It has nothing to do with analytical logic, dogmatic belief, or even speculative metaphysics, but points the way to an experience we can have and, indeed, are meant to have. Once we have had it, we come to see that our earthly existence, between the twin poles of life and death, is rooted in a transcendental state of Being, which forms the hidden ground of our own nature and which we, as human beings, can and must bring to consciousness. But to have this experience and have it validly, we must first discard the old consciousness, which has hardened into habit and determines the way we think and act. What this means as possibility, challenge, path, and consequence, Zen teaches in a manner that is valid not only for the East, but for us Westerners as well. And Zen is particularly important for us today because we, too, must now cross over—assuming we realize that we have reached the crossing point. The Eastern master uses rig-

6

orous practice to bring his student to a point beyond which something wholly different and unexampled beckons, and this is where the general development of the Western spirit has left many of us today. Increasingly, people are coming to an extreme point where they are filled with anger and despair at what they themselves and the world around them have become—but are also aware of something new in themselves, holding the promise of freedom.

As soon as the true self awakes, however, inertia exerts its dead weight, protecting things as they are and preventing us from making the breakthrough—and so the forces of darkness and delay are again at work today, using the sacrosanct traditions of science and religion as a pretext to impede the progress of the new. As usual, the reactionaries' efforts, both overt and covert, are finding support in the huckstering tactics of those who "sell" the new, without understanding it or at too low a price—spreading ideas and practices that are positively harmful and prevent the forces of good, which are breaking through on all sides, from achieving final victory.

The concepts of nothingness and Being, the boundary and the breakthrough, Tao and Zen, are already being bandied about on all sides. The whole thing is discussed, dissected—and above all distorted, since we are given to understand that we can grasp Zen intellectually and make it a part of ourselves without effort or change on our part. This is one way of turning something that is meaningful only when fully lived and practiced into a kind of intellectual parlor game. Generally speaking, we are only too inclined to surrender to the spell of abstract ideas and high-sounding concepts without noticing the highly practical demands they make on us, or in any way relating them to ourselves. This is also the danger if we approach Zen in the wrong way. We must be clear on one point: Zen may look like a speculative system, its ideas and concepts may seem purely abstract to the ignorant or uninitiated—but it is actually concerned, in a real and burning sense, with our own experience in the here-and-now. It touches our lives, with our sufferings and the everlasting cycle of death and rebirth, on the deepest level and penetrates to our real nature, which is only waiting to be discovered and acknowledged. This discovery, if we make it, is the one decisive event in our human existence—the event that breaks all the molds and makes everything over. It is with this event and nothing else that Zen is concerned—with satori, the "great experience," in which Life, which brings us forth and shapes us, which cherishes and everlastingly gives birth to us anew, and which we ourselves are, reveals itself to us and enters our consciousness.

Anyone who has worked hard enough on himself, or whom personal need has left open to receive it, can hope to know satori, which has nothing to do with existing religious beliefs—although its nature undoubtedly places it at the heart of all true religious feeling and so makes it the key to every renewal of religious life. This has always been true, and it holds true today for those who have lost their first, instinctive contact with the basic truths of human life, have shed the beliefs once rooted in those truths and later distorted by theology, and have failed in their efforts to penetrate the mysteries of life by merely rational means.

When it leads us into the truth of life, Zen may take the form of a blossom on the Eastern branch of life's tree—but the experience, wisdom, and practices that it offers are offered to all.

Thus, Zen has universal significance and is not a special religion or *Weltanschauung.* Nor does it try to force alien forms on people who come from other traditions. On the contrary, Zen is a light shining through all of the multicolored windows through which the people and peoples of the earth all try, as their various natures and traditions direct them, to see what lies outside. It is like rain; it lets every seed grow in its own way, but without it every plant dies. It is the earth in which life has all its roots, and in which we must all sink our roots afresh if we want to find the way to ourselves and be renewed. It is the air that every human creature breathes and without which all human life ultimately suffocates.

Zen's Answer to the Problem of Living

In the form in which it reaches us from the East, Zen is often incomprehensible. If it is to help us, we must be able to peel off the alien externals and to separate its general human values, which are what count for us in the West, from the trappings of the East—of Buddhism, Mahayana Buddhism, and even Eastern Zen—all of which may mask its universal truth from us to start with. Even then, we will be able to hear what Zen has to tell us only if we try to approach it not in a spirit of theoretical inquiry, but at the urging of our own vital needs. We shall never understand what Zen is about if we try to break it down into a theory—in other words, if we stand back and try to be objective. From a distance, there is no such thing as Zen.

A loved woman exists fully and has meaning only for the man who loves her, an enemy only for those who fear him, a friend only for those whom his understanding warms, and a healer only for those who seek a cure. In the same way, Zen exists only as a living answer to real-life problems, to the sufferings and longings of individual human beings. If we try to take Zen objectively and to judge it by the standards of logic, ethics, or aesthetics, then we shall simply miss what it has to say, or misunderstand its message completely and reject the whole thing as obscure and abstruse. Whenever we try to force the inexplicable into an image or a concept, we are really trying to tame it and make it familiar—and there is always a danger that its real and vital meaning will be lost.

Westerners tend to be the prisoners of their own rationality, and there is something grotesque and naïve about the way in which they boldly pass judgment on religions—including their own—in terms that strip them of any real meaning. All that is left is the shell—images, observances, words, and empty concepts—reflecting something that was felt and thought long ago, but is now parted from its living source and has become lifeless and misleading. A living religion (and a religion is only real when it lives) is always an answer to the vital needs and longings of mankind. Religion can neither exist nor be understood in any other way. But today one has the feeling that many of the guardians of religion—the churches and churchmen—are themselves deeply alienated from the real meaning of the "doctrines" they profess. Otherwise, they would hardly see the unearthing of a link between the revelation imprisoned in dogma and conventional practice and the vital foundations of belief in personal feeling and experience as a dangerous attempt to subjectivize something objective—as if the superhuman and transcendental elements in religion had no roots and counterparts in human beings themselves.

To remain a force for action in the human heart, religion must be directly relevant to life, and to the sufferings and aspirations that give life its shape, for this is the only area in which religion is meaningful, valid, and vital. When revelation no longer speaks to the human heart, it becomes a doctrine and depends on the leap of faith for credibility—or it becomes a worldview and holds true only as long as reason accepts it. How else could millions of our own contemporaries have lost their so-called faith because they can no longer reconcile things that have happened to themselves or others with their rational-ethical notions of divine order and the justice of God?

There are plenty of wrongheaded ideas about faith, and most of them are rooted in the assumption that religion is objectively true and universally valid, has nothing to do with the way people really feel, think, and react, and needs to be protected against the "merely subjective" element in individual experience. But all of this misses the point on three counts:

1. We need the distinction between the objective (conceptually definable) and the subjective (colored by personal feelings and desires) as long as we are dealing with verifiable facts—but here we are shifting into an area where there are no objective or scientific facts, where the "real" is only real insofar as it exists in an individual consciousness and provokes an individual reaction.

2. If we reject all religious experience as merely subjective, we are forgetting that religious experience—like every other personal experience—falls into two basic categories: the relative and purely individual experience of a particular person in a particular time and place; and personal experience that comes from the individual's real center, from his inmost nature, where time and place do not apply. This kind of experience is not psychologically determined—though the images we use to convey it and the words we use to interpret it may be—and it is not, therefore, "merely subjective." Essentially, it bears witness to humanity's transcendental nature, which, since humanity consists of individuals, can speak only through a particular person in a particular time and place. Whenever humanity's true nature—i.e., the mode in which divine Being is present in all of us—speaks out like this from the depths, its words have a validity beyond time. How else could the sayings of the sages and great mystics, all the way back to Lao-tse, continue to touch the hearts of those wise enough to hear them with their timeless truths?

3. There is a third reason why the idea that individual experience can reflect a supernatural, transcendent reality is not taken seriously or is even discounted altogether. Christian theology has always kept the terms *supernatural* and *transcendent* for a divine reality totally beyond human ken—and this means that they are not available to describe even the most profound of human experiences, which are thought of as being "intrapsychic" and thus at a vast remove from the transcendent. Without entering into theological argument, it must still be said that human experience undoubtedly can encompass something that wholly outstrips natural reason and its power to comprehend. This kind of experience feels entirely different and floods us with a mysterious energy; indeed, the whole thing is so overwhelmingly unlike even the most striking of our everyday experiences that if we call the one physical, natural, human, and worldly, we have no choice but to call the other metaphysical, supernatural, otherworldly, and transcendent. We shall leave it an open question whether these

experiences are pre-theological (the product of natural piety and thus of less value than theological truth) or whether theology, which has the duality of all verbal systems (logos), is not surpassed utterly by the realities revealed to us in mystical experience. One thing, however, is sure: we can only make contact with the transcendental truths of Zen if our own experience, our own anguish, leaves us open to receive it, and if we can see it as an answer to that anguish—or as the fulfillment of an inner promise. If Zen is to work for us, the first question is, "What is the anguish and what are the longings of people in the West to which Zen today holds the answer?"

Western Humanity—
Anguish and
an End to Anguish

Suffering and Promise — the Sources of the Quest

It is suffering, above all, that gives human beings no rest, keeps them on the move, and drives them on unceasingly. "Mark it well, all you who ponder and are given to reflection, your swiftest steed on the path to perfection is suffering," said Meister Eckhart.

If suffering sets people searching, then relief from suffering is what they are looking for, and there is a clear implication that this goal can be reached, the cause of suffering found, and suffering itself eliminated.

There are three basic things that make people suffer. The first is the constant threat of annihilation, the terrifying uncertainty of life and its transience, which makes them long for permanence, security, something solid to hold on to. The second is despair at life's meaninglessness, which makes them look for a permanent meaning. The third is a sense of the fearful insecurity of life, which makes them look for a place of permanent safety. At first, people rely on their own strength and try to find stability, meaning, and security in the world around them. But they are bound to fail, and when they do, they turn for peace to the stillness of divine Being, where fear, despair, and sorrow are healed from another direction.

But if people are tormented by the impermanence, meaninglessness, and desolation of the everyday world, and look outside it for a cure, this surely suggests that there is some deep-seated intuition promising them something else, something that they can experience directly and that eliminates uncertainty, senselessness, and insecurity by offering them permanence, meaning, and safety from another source—something that is not, in fact, of this world. The truth is that to be human is not simply to be an ego, to be rooted in this world and depend on it; it is also to operate on a far deeper level as the medium through which Being seeks to manifest itself in the world, and thus to have a share in Being oneself. This is why the suffering inflicted by the world and the longing to be free of it are not the only cause of human anguish. Another is loss of the ability to serve as a medium for Being, i.e., loss of contact and union with the Absolute in ourselves. But suffering is not the only thing that drives human beings on into the divine haven where wanderings cease, a home anchor beckons, and fear, despair, and sorrow are at last laid to rest. If we respond to the suffering that cries out within us for relief, we respond even more profoundly to the divine life that animates our innermost being and is constantly seeking to manifest itself in us as fullness, form, and unity, in a never-ending process of change and creation. This is the source of the wholly new energy that drives us forward—the energy that springs from the promise felt within, and the longing for ultimate fulfillment it generates.

If it is true that a promise provides our real impetus, then our goal is not redemption, but fulfillment of that promise—a fulfillment in which vitality, beauty, and unity are all perfected: not redemption from a life filled with sorrow, but awakening to a new life; not existence fading into the stasis of Being, but Being creatively manifest in the multiple forms and order of existence. It is true that this is a Western, not an Eastern, a Christian, not a Buddhist way of looking at things. But the way to this fulfillment leads across a common threshold: satori, the great experience.

The three components of human happiness are vitality, beauty, and a sheltering sense of community. We always start by relying on ourselves and looking for these three things in power, order, and fellowship as the world understands them. Failing to find them there, we eventually seek them in the only way that makes sense—in Being, which transforms, fulfills, and brings us to new life.

Turning to Being is turning inward, but turning inward for fulfillment would surely be a futile exercise unless what we found there was, in some sense, absolute and totally divorced from the agonizing ego-world complex in which we are entangled to start with.

And so people today, bitterly conscious of the imperfections of existence, are driven on by two factors in their search for something better: an overpowering sense of the world's relativity and the sense of a hidden absolute—a promise deep within themselves.

The way forward leads from the anguish rooted in the old self to the experience of what we really are, and from the experience of what we really are to fulfillment in a new self; it leads through the death of the old self to the birth of a new self from what we truly are—i.e., to the true self.

Zen knows about redemptive Being and the life that springs from it. Zen knows about our inner nature, in which Being is present within us, offering us salvation and the genuine hope of a new life that will transform and remake us. Zen knows about the wall that cuts us off from Being, and it knows how we can tear it down. But we shall understand Zen only if we can hear within ourselves what Zen, in its own way, is saying. To receive the gift that Zen offers us, we must first ask ourselves, What is the anguish, the human anguish, that afflicts us today? And what are the signs that promise us that it will end?

The Shackles of
Objective Consciousness

Our problems in the West begin when one particular form of consciousness—itself a necessary stage in human development—takes complete hold and dominates all others. This is *objective consciousness*, which makes us see reality as something "objective," that is, something existing without reference to ourselves, and makes us apply the yardstick of "objectivity" to everything we do. Bravely setting out to understand, control, or shape the world around us, we discount our own aspirations and desires as "merely subjective." But succeeding or failing only in terms of an "objective" reality is precisely what human life is not about. Indeed, human life is primarily a matter of experiencing, transforming, and fulfilling—or failing to fulfill—ourselves subjectively, and joy and pain tell us if, and where, we are living in or out of line with our deeper nature's promise and potential. Where and how is that deeper nature, our innermost core, to become real if not in our *subjective* selves and *subjective* experience? If we sacrifice the claims not only of our puny egos, but also of our true nature to those of a supposedly "objective" world, and deny and repress our subjective selves in the name of a life that can manifest and fulfill itself only in "objective" systems, then we ultimately fail to make contact with ourselves and plunge into a kind of pain that is particularly and peculiarly human. Failure to grasp the meaning of Buddhism, and indeed Oriental wisdom in general, is synonymous with a failure to grasp the nature of this pain and to recognize the danger that threatens us all if we let this type of consciousness, which objectivizes everything, take over. The saving doctrines of Buddhism and of Zen see this danger for what it is and know how to save us from the anguish it causes.

Objective consciousness and its systems and values have a far firmer hold on the Western than on the Eastern mind, and this is why the manifestations of the Eastern spirit often strike the Westerner as alien and diffuse. But as soon as the Westerner starts to realize that his ways of thinking and perceiving are incomplete, and to be made uncomfortable by that fact, the promise latent in the Eastern spirit begins to cast its spell.

The universal truth embodied in Zen is no less accessible to the Westerner rooted in Christian belief than it is to the Easterner—but we are genuinely receptive to it only when we personally feel the anguish and danger that Zen sets out to remove. This is why we cannot make fruitful contact with Zen until we understand what objective consciousness is, why it is dangerous, and why it makes us suffer.

Asked to say what reality is, a Westerner automatically responds from the part of his subjective nature that is rooted in the objective, defining ego, using concepts belonging to a consciousness conditioned by Kant's space-time categories and also rooted in the ego. This is completely natural for us, but by no means completely natural for everyone. An educated Easterner—even a scientist who has just spoken of reality in terms dictated by that ego—will instantly "think again" if asked to say what reality *really* is and attempt to answer from the part of his subjective being that is rooted not in the ego, but in Tao- or Buddha-nature, i.e., in his "true" nature. And what will he say? He may simply smile and say nothing, or he may reply in symbols, images, and paradoxes that mean nothing to us. If he has to say something, however, he will surprise us by saying, first of all, that the reality perceived by the reflective ego is itself an illusion, masking the "true nature" of all reality, which can never be grasped conceptually. Our surprise results from the fact that we Westerners identify instinctively and utterly with the self of everyday consciousness and no longer realize that the image of reality imprinted on that consciousness is extremely limited, that it misses the reality of Being and is transcended by it. It is at this point that we must turn to epistemology for a clearer picture of what objective consciousness is.

What Objective Consciousness Is—Why It Is Dangerous

The objective vision of life is grounded in the *ego*—the ego that is meant when we say "I am I." The *principle of identity* thus lies at the heart of objective consciousness and its vision of reality. When a person thinks of himself, he thinks of something he identifies with himself—something standing fast amid the flux of events. This self-anchored ego provides the standpoint from which he sees the world around him, and its consciousness defines what he sees by asking, "What is that?" and replying, "It is such-and-such," thus congealing life into *facts,* which are fixed and to which he must cling. Everything perceived and experienced is seen from the standpoint of the self and related to the self—and becomes, as it were, the anti-self. The world is something that can be—or has been—defined and understood objectively, and things are "real" only to the extent that they are rooted in this objective reality, which is itself pinned down in *concepts.* This means that nothing is real unless it has been—or can be—integrated within a conceptual system. If it cannot be integrated within such a system, it is either not real yet or has stopped being real. It is merely "subjective"—the stuff of images, fancies, beliefs, feelings, and desires.

The person who is identified with his defining ego and anchored in objective consciousness is affected in two ways: first, he has a special way of seeing, a "theory" concerning what is to be regarded as real and assumed to be so; and, second, he takes a special, pragmatic view of the world, sorting it into what counts and does not count for him. Looking at it, he accepts as real only things that he sees as having a definite existence "outside" himself. In the same way, the only thing that makes him real himself is having a definite *standpoint* and sticking to it—and this standpoint determines the positive or negative significance of everything else.

Objectivity in general has nothing to do with physical objects, but is one of the ways in which things are brought to consciousness and anchored in it. It has its own type of consciousness, and this is governed by the ego, the self that defines the anti-self and registers objects ("objects of consciousness") only in counterpoint to itself. This is why *antitheses* are another feature of this consciousness. Seeing itself as something that it equates with itself, the ego sees everything else as something that it contrasts with itself, generating the typical *subject/object duality* of objective consciousness. Similarly, whenever the ego sees something as having a definite existence, it also marks it off from other things around it (it is "this" and not "that"), thus immediately breaking the whole of perceived reality down not simply into objects, but into antithetical objects. Antitheses, like objectivity, are a basic feature of the reality constructed by the defining ego. The consciousness that perceives objectively and operates with antitheses or dualisms stands and falls—like the reality in which it deals—with the self-anchored ego. "Here/there," "before/after," "above/below" exist only in relation to the fixed ego at the heart of consciousness and the reality perceived by that ego. And so we see that space and time are the natural ordering principles of the self-defining, all-defining ego's worldview, and pertain solely to the way in which life is brought to consciousness in relation to that ego. But what happens if this ego disappears?

The person identified with his ego naturally sees the reality presented to him by that ego as the whole of reality, and dismisses as unreal anything that has not been made, or cannot be made, to fit in with it. Anything that affects him and cannot be objectively defined—feelings, beliefs, experiences too deeply felt for words—must be labeled and made to fit the system before it can be acknowledged. At best, it constitutes a kind of preliminary form of objective consciousness, the only consciousness with the authority to process reality "as it is." Similarly, the only licensed subject of perception is the perceiving ego embodied in that consciousness. There is nothing outside the ego, and if the ego goes, he assumes that the whole of reality—and he himself—will go with it. This view of life offers no escape from the pain of imprisonment in objective consciousness. It is the way people think when they have no subjective existence outside the ego; but they are wrong, and the spiritual anguish of even educated Westerners is only deepened by their "natural" tendency to think in these terms. Recognition of this error is one of the basic features of all Eastern wisdom. Eliminating it and teaching the way that leads out of anguish are the central and universally significant concern of Zen.

The West says, If this ego ceases to be, then meaningful reality disappears with it. But the East says, It is not until this ego and the reality it has shaped cease to be that humanity's "true nature" is released and true reality dawns—and only from this reality can the essential, the greater, the true self emerge.

Zen says that, far from "nothing" being left when a person drops his normal ego—and he can drop it—the whole of life is present in a different way, that is, it is *really* present for the first time. The individual ceases to be a subject perceiving the world solely as a multiplicity of defined objects, and becomes a subject in whom life comes internally to consciousness as something transcending objects and antitheses. This new vision depends on a widening of the consciousness, a qualitative leap that everyone must make at a certain point in his development—the leap that takes us from life writ small into Life writ large, from the relative into the Absolute, from what we naturally are into what enlightenment can make us— people whose lives are rooted in a new knowledge. Enlightenment opens the door to the secret. What secret? Our own inner nature, hidden at first from the worldly ego's gaze, in which supra-worldly Being dwells within us. It is with this leap into Being that Zen is concerned.

The time to make the leap has come when Being, which is present within us to start with, sustaining and nurturing us without any effort on our part, has been wholly dominated and obscured by objective consciousness. This is precisely the point many of us have reached today, but it is also the point where we in the West have one major problem and challenge to confront: to free our true nature, we must question a way of seeing that not only colors and shapes our whole awareness of the world, but has also given us our finest achievements, the outstanding achievements of Western science and technology. How can we resolve this dilemma?

Long ago, our medieval ancestors had to break through the fog of hallowed images of reality constructed by the pre-rational mind, which prevented the rational mind from seeing that reality plainly. The breakthrough brought into existence the new human being, self-reliant, unprejudiced, observing nature at a distance and using rational concepts to measure it objectively, ultimately bringing it under his control. And now the time has come to open another new era by dispelling the fog of another fixed system and striking forward into the open, for the new world before us today is partly hidden by the very energies that produced the last era and made it great—but have now hardened into a straitjacket. Today, the rational mind is the barrier. Science plumbing the depths of nature, technology literally storming the heavens, our universal organizing talents, and all the other things of which we in the West are justly proud—all of this has left us with a blinkered regard for the rational consciousness to which we owe it all, so that anything that consciousness cannot grasp immediately seems dubious. But now the new values that hold the key to the future are bursting from the other side of human nature, the side that reason cannot penetrate. There are more signs than we suspect that the new era is dawning. More people than we realize are having experiences in which their true nature speaks to them, experiences that disturb and gladden them by suddenly bringing them the sense of a new reality outside the one they know—a reality charged with saving energy, filled with promise and making new demands on them. It is no longer understanding and controlling the objective, tangible world that counts here, but seeing the truth of transcendent nature, which is present in us and in the world around us and, once it comes to consciousness, transforms our lives and gives them wholly new horizons. But who can teach us Westerners to pay attention, before it is too late, to the experiences in which this nature speaks to us?

Here lies the significance of Zen. Everything Zen says breathes the air of the other, greater reality that opens out before us when we throw off the shackles of objective consciousness. Everything Zen does centers on taking these experiences seriously. They themselves are never the product of abstract speculation, but burst unexpectedly from the darkness of existential anguish or the glimmering dawn of existential promise, on the outermost edge of what can still be rationally grasped. All of Zen's practical exercises are meant to prepare us for these experiences, which transcend the old boundaries, but to see what they are really aiming at, we must take a closer look at the ways in which the objective view of reality actually affects human life.

The Pain of Living

When objective consciousness rules a person's thinking, his chief aim in life is to assert himself by acquiring wealth, prestige, and power. It is vital—and not only for the purpose of understanding Zen—to realize that self-assertive practice and "objective" theory have the same starting point: the ego constantly concerned with ensuring its own survival and defending its own position.

If this ego *is* the individual, the individual not only sees the world around him as a fixed system of facts, giving him something to hold on to and steer by; he also sees himself as the natural center of existence as he lives it, i.e., as an ego with a right to be—and remain—what it is.

If this ego *is* the individual, the individual not only says "I am I," but adds "I shall remain I." Basically, he sees everything else in counterpoint to that "I," either confirming or contesting its will to remain what it is, either prepared to go along with it or willfully standing apart. He never says yes to anything—however much he stands to gain in a personal, developmental sense from doing so—without first making it clear that his will to remain what he is must not be tampered with.

The greatest threat to the ego is constant change, the apparent impermanence of everything, and, finally, death. The ground-notes of existence—the constant threat of extinction, meaninglessness, and vulnerability—fundamentally center on one thing: the individual's determination to preserve himself in circumstances that are safe, make sense, and allow him to live in security with others. Existence is acceptable only if every danger has been removed from it, meaningful only if it runs its course among secure meaning and value systems. Above all, he wants things to be definite—and he wants to keep what he has. This is why he clings to his attitudes, resists external change, holds on to his possessions, and, even in the realm of thought and knowledge, hangs on to his opinions once he has arrived at them. Enmeshed in fixed concepts, he wants life to be a cross between a cottage and a castle, combining security with comfort and allowing him to bask in the esteem of others like himself and quietly give himself up to the enjoyment of his own company and anything else that keeps him happy. Even when he takes up a cause and sacrifices his purely selfish ego for a thing, project, or community, he assumes that something lasting—a cause, a community, or even a value system—is at stake. Objective consciousness can indeed produce selfless effort as well as naked self-assertion—as long as that effort serves something "objective." At the center of this physically safe, intellectually meaningful, and spiritually reassuring vision of life, the individual identified with his world-ego can hold out indefinitely.

So far, so good, but the bill refuses to add up, because this is not what life is like and because the main item is missing. The main item in human life is never the ego circling a fixed point, but an inner nature from and through which a greater life seeks to manifest itself in constant change, extending to everything and including the ego. A person imprisoned in his ego is like a caterpillar dreaming of heaven—not just a heaven without feet to trample it, but a heaven without butterflies either, although the butterfly is the caterpillar's hidden meaning and is fated to explode its present form. Inner nature can manifest itself only in constant change, but the ego and its will to remain what it is make change impossible, always circling a fixed point—even when the fixed point is nothing more than the code that determines how people in a given community behave. This is how one specific type of human anguish starts. And this anguish increases as the individual inexorably falls victim to a world he himself has willed into being: the rationally ordered, ethically determined, and technically regulated world in which we live today, the world that has exhausted our inner resources and now threatens to crush us.

Depersonalization of the Individual

Being is the animating force in everything that lives, and it provides a threefold impetus: every living thing seeks to live; every living thing seeks not merely to live, but to become fully and uniquely itself; and every living thing seeks to fulfill itself in transcendent totality. This threefold urge is innate and universal, and in it we sense the vital plenitude of Being that generates, sustains, and renews everything that is. In it we see the regularity and order of inherent form underlying the full spectrum of individual phenomena. In it we feel the unity of Being in which everything is ultimately one—the unity from which everything sprang and to which it is constantly striving to return.

When Being enters consciousness and while it remains, it gives us a basic strength and confidence in life, it bears witness to our true nature, it expresses faith in a universal order matching that nature, and it lends us the security that comes from feeling part of a wider whole and from peace of heart. But as the ego gradually asserts itself and weakens our contact with Being, the unconscious forces that so far have supported, shielded, and given meaning to existence are transformed into conscious intentions and desires, for example, the desire for security in an existence where we respond to the world as we see it by relying on what we ourselves know, own, and can do; the desire to shape and order things in patterns that make sense to us; and the desire for human fellowship and the comfort it offers. The Absolute was our first home, but we now move into a new, relative structure that we have built ourselves and that makes us feel secure because we know how it works and why it works the way it does.

By living exclusively in this new system and accepting only what squares with it, however, we start to push Being even further away, and our true nature increasingly drops out of consciousness. As we identify with, become enslaved by, and hide behind artifacts and systems of our own devising, we are increasingly in danger of being devoured by them. Today this process is affecting people in three ways: victimized by impersonal systems of their own creation, they are turning into objects themselves; they are being forced to repress their individuality; they are no longer allowed to take their own transcendental dimension seriously.

There is less and less room today for individuals with their own sufferings and aspirations toward happiness and meaning—individuals who run their own lives and demand the freedom to do so; for as life is depersonalized, the individual himself is turned into a thing, a component, an object. He is seen as a thing and treated like a thing, and must live like a thing. Even the sciences that study him, such as conventional

27

medicine and psychology, narrow their focus to what can be rationally defined and grasped, to what can be turned into a thing. Wherever he is, and particularly at work, he is at the mercy of the organized world around him—a minor cog in the meshes of a machine that is omnipotent and omnipresent and cares only for output and order. All his functions are measurable, and he himself is reduced to simple functioning, like another machine. The fact that he is not a thing, but a human being, with his own life, his own sufferings, his own aspirations, and his own claim to be fully himself, matters nothing to the objective systems and the people who run them—or matters only when his personal problems threaten to upset the smoothly running system that he is expected to serve, and serve productively.

A person's humanity is enormously reduced when he becomes a mere object of rational knowledge, part of a fixed system, the source of an output that can be objectively measured. To get ahead, he must let his "soul" go; to serve as an interchangeable spare part, he must sacrifice his own individuality. In short, he must "adjust" to the needs of a totally organized world in which everything is expected to run without a hitch. Deep down, however, he can only "adjust" if a life without problems has genuinely become his own supreme ambition. Once this happens, once a superficially trouble-free existence becomes the main target, running away from pain and suffering seems entirely reasonable, and anything that drowns out and screens the suffering inherent in human life becomes acceptable. But to live like this is to miss the truth of life, and living a lie can lead to sickness and anguish. Even sickness and anguish, however, are rapidly relieved in a civilization that increasingly resembles an enormous factory churning out remedies to enable people to keep going wrong— painlessly. Their pain is there to tell them that they have gone wrong, but instead of reading the symptoms and changing direction, they surrender their freedom to shape their own lives, and chase the mirage of a life that seems serene, but is totally lacking in transcendental depth. The person who strikes this kind of bargain with the world and lives out his life without a care has no further need of God and ultimately feels free—but only because he is no longer aware of his chains. The claims of his own true nature and his roots in transcendent Being are forgotten. But in spite of everything, his true nature is still there, as his real center and the medium through which the Absolute is striving to manifest itself in him. He is dimly conscious of an inner struggle, and his life—unless he realizes what is happening and rises to the challenge—is governed by a lie. If this makes him suffer and if any of his childhood beliefs have survived, he asks God for the strength to continue living in this lie—and thinks that he is showing humility when he is really only running away from himself.

To get rid of personal values, and particularly personal aspirations, to objectify everything, to lose individuality and to deny transcendent Being—this is to strike at the wholeness and essence of the human condition. This is what happens when existence becomes completely worldly or "secularized," and we lose sight of supra-worldly Being, which holds the key to real existence, which we are meant to manifest, and whose transforming, gladdening, and mandatory inner presence is the only thing that can save us.

But it is only the sight of it that we lose, for basically every human being always remains what he is, a personal, individual subject, rooted in transcendence. This is why his true nature, if constantly repressed, still makes its presence felt and ultimately raises the standard of revolt. Everything that is done to turn a person into a thing only brings him closer to the day when he inevitably realizes that real life starts when he opens the door to personal values. Only constant denial of his individuality really makes him start to sense its rightful claims. He sees that the rationalization of life has sacrificed the feminine to the masculine element in the human makeup and that this feminine element must be restored—and he also sees that human individuality has an absolute right to fulfillment. When this right is denied, the individual sickens; he is tormented by feelings of fear, shame, and desolation for which he can find no obvious cause. The suppressed forces of his deeper nature erupt and turn against him without his realizing it, finding a variety of self-destructive, self-damaging outlets. Angst is a common symptom today, and is always a sign that a person's inner nature is choking for air. As the transcendental roots of their humanity slip from consciousness, and as the secret but unchanging claims of that dimension cease to find satisfaction in forms of belief that have also been turned into things, people increasingly become the victims of the unholy world they themselves have created. At last, when the pain grows unbearable, when they can no longer run from themselves, they must listen to the voice from within, look closely at inner experiences that they have previously ignored, and search for paths leading to a new system of belief. In the fullest sense, this process brings people back to themselves. It is powerfully under way today—and gaining added momentum from the fact that the emphasis on things and organization has also robbed the communities in which people live and the jobs they do of the central, hallowed element that once gave them something solid, meaningful, and safe to hold on to.

The Decline of Community

The individual claims of a person's inner nature pass unnoticed as long as he remains part of a privileged whole, an organic community that supports him, gives his life meaning, and offers him security. His deeper aspirations are subsumed in the aspirations of the whole community, and his personal nature is not denied, even if the community ignores his purely personal concerns. When he is truly a part of the community, the community lives subjectively in him. What it is determines how he behaves, and the ways in which he interrelates and coexists with others have value and meaning for him and for them in terms of the life they share within it. By identifying with it, he knows—even when he is forced to repress his own wishes—that he is fulfilling himself in a way that, if not yet personal, is still entirely human. It is only when the community breaks up and is replaced by an impersonal "collective," when the organic becomes the organized, and when objective, pragmatic values are the only ones that count, that everything changes. Rated solely in terms of output and efficiency and ignored as a "person," the individual no longer has any references outside himself, and the basic meaning of his life—now a matter of concern to him alone—becomes a problem he must confront and solve for himself. As society increasingly moves in this direction, educating people solely to take their places as productive components in objective systems, their inner natures are driven into contradiction and rebellion while they are still young. Young people—and even children—find themselves facing inner problems that simply do not exist as long as family life remains vigorous and stable. Self-fulfillment becomes a matter of vital importance at a very early age, and the young are thrown into hopeless confusion.

Painless integration within the community and gradual absorption of its values, ethics, and rules of conduct used to be the norm—but this is now being replaced by rigid conformity and the forced acceptance of ideals, standards, and conventions that seem less and less convincing and can no longer be lived by as a matter of course. If a person is still instinctively referring to the things told him in childhood and to the old standards and beliefs, serious inner conflicts develop when he eventually has to fend for himself. He senses that the time has come to strike out on his own and to give his insistent true nature its head, but feels guilty—either because he is betraying the standards originally dinned into him or, if he sticks to them, because he is betraying himself. When this point is reached—and countless people have reached it today—there is no going back. The only way is forward, bravely forward to the one true source of personal existence and personal decision. This source is nothing other than the *realm of personal experience* and the unmistakable voice of humanity's true nature that speaks from it. Obviously, when objective values that have lost credibility are rejected, instincts and urges normally

31

checked in organic communities are likely to break through. It goes without saying that they must be subordinated to the community's code, consideration for others, and spiritual obligations—although the real conflict now is no longer between instinctive egoism and altruism, but between loyalty to the community and fulfillment of the individual's true nature. The rebellion of the young already prefigures the rebellion of true nature—the new self that has come to maturity and insists on being acknowledged and seen for what it is. The first, decisive step toward this maturity is taken by turning to *supernatural experience,* as people today are doing—paying attention to those experiences in which true nature, the medium in which the Absolute is present and seeks to manifest itself in us, speaks as challenge and as promise.

This experience comes as the climax of a maturing process in which we first go astray and lose contact with our true nature, but eventually find our way back to it and hear once again the voice of wisdom from our own inner depths. It is Zen's purpose to bring these depths to consciousness.

Portents of Change

From Natural to Supernatural Experience

The suppression of our true nature is the surest path to the deepest pit of human suffering—and out of this suffering is suddenly born the longing to find a way back to a life infused with that true nature. Yesterday we still took it for granted that our business in life was to master the world and find our place in it; today this aim is no longer enough. It seems too narrow, too superficial, once we have sensed the presence of something deeper within: the true, the supra-worldly life, inexorably forcing its way toward the light. This life never stands still, but is changing all the time, and any fixed system deflects its vital impulse. Whenever this happens, a strange unrest takes hold, inexplicable feelings of fear, guilt, and emptiness, which none of the everyday remedies can cure. We may be secure, but the fear persists. We may be living virtuously, but the guilt is still there. We may be rich, but the emptiness remains. The real problem lies in another direction.

The sense of longing felt by people today conceals the hidden knowledge of a fullness that flows from humanity's true nature, which itself depends on nothing and can break our own dependence on all the things placed within the worldly ego's grasp by wealth, position, and power. It is the knowledge of a meaning beyond meaning or unmeaning, justice or injustice, as the ego understands those terms; knowledge of the inner self, ceaselessly revealing itself in an ever-changing pattern of forms that merge into and flow from one another; knowledge of security born of a love that has nothing to do with human love and breaks our dependence on that love—a love that takes all the heartache out of solitude. This hidden knowledge underlies the great longing, and in it our *true nature* is at work. In it, Being is present within us in a way that makes us strangely independent of all the things clung to by the world-centered, world-dependent ego. It is a knowledge that has nothing to do with the ordinary logic of objective consciousness, and makes nonsense of that logic's smug claim to be the only logic that counts. We first sense it dimly on the outer rim of consciousness. Later, we feel it as a promise. Later still, we hear it as a voice; and this voice grows steadily clearer, more hopeful, and more challenging. We are filled with a new sense of purpose and at last start to see the importance of the times when this knowledge first flickered within us or—even more powerfully—was briefly present as a certainty. It is only at this point that we can recognize the real turning points in our lives, the glorious moments when Being speaks to us, but that we dismiss as unreal, as long as we cling to tangibles. It is only at this point that we are willing to listen to those who have had these sensations before us, have recognized their importance, and have made them the first step on a way where this momentary experience is progressively revealed as the one true reality. At this point we are also ready for the wisdom of the East, which has never stopped listening for the voice of hidden knowledge—and obeying it as an infallible guide to the inner way.

This is the central difference between the culture of the East and the civilization of the West: the keynote in the West is *form*—the form that a person imposes on the world (objective systems) and on himself (personality); the keynote in the East is *maturity*—maturity reached by following the way that every human being must take to become a person in the fullest sense. This way is the way of inner experience—of *transcendence present within us*—and the new era is heralding itself by focusing on that experience.

The Western mind has thus far rested on two pillars: rational knowledge derived from natural sense-data, and a belief in supernatural revelation. The East, which has nothing equivalent to Christian belief and has never looked to pure reason for an explanation of life's meaning and purpose, finds true knowledge and the key to human nature as it really is in something else: supernatural experience and natural revelation. This insight comes only when we have gone beyond the limits of our natural powers, and helps us only if we are prepared to take inner experience seriously and let the inner voice guide us. It has two components, the conviction that there is a higher reality that commands belief, and the conviction that we can already sense this reality as something present within us in the here-and-now. It was long regarded as the private property either of the East or of a privileged few in the West, but is now coming slowly to general awareness and has even—in moments of shattering illumination—become for many people a personal certainty. Westerners, no less than Easterners, have fateful moments when Being comes to life within them—but Westerners have not thus far been taught to understand what is happening and see its importance. This is where Zen can help them—can help *us*.

What are these fateful moments? They are the times when something deeper unexpectedly touches us and lifts us suddenly into another reality. This experience can come, like an all-transforming light, when our world is darkened by suffering, and it can come, suddenly casting an otherworldly radiance over everything, when we have reached a peak of worldly happiness. It can come when our strength, wisdom, and spiritual endurance are exhausted and we despair—if we accept that despair and see that the new self that emerges when the old one collapses is what we really are. It sometimes comes when annihilation threatens, when we can suddenly look death in the face without flinching and feel a new, unknown life within us—giving us the inexplicable conviction that we cannot be harmed, that we can do anything. It sometimes comes when we are filled with despair at life's meaninglessness or with a crushing sense of our own guilt. If we can accept the unacceptable, if we can endure the unendurable, then—as we accept, as we endure, and as our strength burns lower—we may suddenly experience an inner light that illuminates us utterly, that has nothing to do with understanding a particular thing, but that shifts the whole basis of our understanding. Sometimes it also comes when we accept loneliness or helplessness of an intensity that threatens our very survival; even as it gnaws at our vital substance, we may have a sudden sense of being cherished and protected on a deeper level, of being rooted in an intimate relationship with something we cannot define. This is the age-old experience of the essential *unity* of all things in Being, in which every person has a share. This sudden, inexplicable sense of being firmly anchored in power, clarity, and love is an expression of the mystery that is being revealed in humanity itself—the mystery of Being, in whose fullness, order, and unity the whole of existence is rooted and is constantly renewing itself as life, meaning, and security.

Who can tell how often the horrors of battlefield, air raid, prison, and death camp—in short, the darkest moments—have brought people face to face with the divine power within themselves, suddenly flooding them with light at the moment of ultimate disaster? This is modern humanity's hidden treasure: the experience of something "utterly different," which has enabled countless men and women not only to endure the unendurable, but also to bear witness to true nature, which is only waiting to be recognized, heard, and let in. How many people have felt the strength that comes when death seems certain—and is humbly accepted? How many have seen understanding dawn from despair when they have stopped looking for reasons and accepted what they cannot comprehend? How many have felt the inexplicable security into which ultimate loneliness can turn when the unbearable is borne? But how few have known what all this meant—although many have been left with a new hope, a new faith, and a new determination to search out the way to the life and the truth that are humanity's true heritage. Zen knows what all this means, and Zen knows about this way.

Thus we see that there are three factors driving Westerners into themselves and helping them to see the treasures of inner experience: the anguish caused by depersonalization in an object-centered society, the destruction of the community that once sheltered and supported the individual, and the horrors we have all lived through in recent decades. Out of all this comes the feeling—and for some the certainty—that there is another dimension we can experience and that can give life in this world a more-than-worldly meaning.

A person thrown back on himself encounters an inner reality that remains hidden as long as he believes that leading a full life is merely a matter of getting on and getting through. It is only when the crisis comes, when life leads him to the edge of the abyss, plunges him into misery and despair, and leaves him more alone than he has ever been before, that he really starts to think about himself and to notice that, deep inside, something new is struggling into consciousness. Coming face to face with his true nature, he experiences something that is not of this world and yet makes him what he is—and its coming to consciousness carries absolute conviction. All of these signs mark the threshold that today's generation is preparing to cross—if it knows which way the future lies.

There are many different areas in which this new experience is reflected: existentialism, abstract art, psychotherapy, modern literature, and, above all, the widespread interest in meditation exercises and the inner way (an interest that has nothing to do with restoring or improving practical performance). It is the young, with their new ideas and new ways of doing things, who are most obviously breaking away from patterns of thought, creativity, behavior, and community living that are fossilized and obsolete. People everywhere are starting to find Being in everyday existence—and releasing their own creative energies in the process. New art forms give us the visible evidence, but on a far deeper level, we can sense that contemporary anguish is finding a positive outlet in people themselves and sending them out in search of something new.

New Wine in Old Bottles

People always approach the unfamiliar in traditional ways. But new wine is always spoiled by old bottles, and so the meaning of the new something toward which people are groping—often without knowing exactly what it is—is being travestied. Many of them are genuinely weary of the world, but the spirit in which they turn to exercise to unlock inner experience is still ruled by the world and the ego.

Small groups and associations are mushrooming on all sides under leaders of varying wisdom and ability, who claim that their exercises will release the adept from his old consciousness and give his life a new meaning. Exercises of all kinds are being urged on the public under respectable names: yoga, meditation, self-exploration, and relaxation therapy. But all too often these activities are more likely to cut people off from the very thing they are passionately seeking than to help them find it. Stress-relieving exercises often degenerate into a cult of "letting go." In the same way, exercises used to shed the old self and find a new one are easily perverted into mere pleasure in release—which does no good and may actually do harm. For example, many people find today that certain "exercises" give them a temporary sense of release from their old identities, but never go beyond this first sensation. Of course, contact with the saving ground of true unity may be a part of this experience, but nothing comes of it unless the new spiritual energies are channeled and consciously centered on a new life and wholehearted practice; otherwise the only result is a cult of experience that is actually incompatible with Being. The exercise becomes a damaging passport to pleasure. Used like a drug to procure the same agreeable sensations over and over again, it substitutes for—and wastes—something that can only come slowly, from bedrock experience and painful, unremitting practice.

Equally dangerous are those relaxation exercises that lull a person into false, unproductive, slothful repose—practically anesthetizing him in the process. These have nothing to do with genuine tranquility of spirit or with the dynamic stillness we register as life-source and challenge, that links us with the divine. They generate a lifeless calm, which certainly makes a pleasant change from angst and agitation, but which distorts instead of releasing the creative energies of life.

A third danger comes when the presence of Being is first sensed, if the meaning of those first contacts—release from the old ego—is reversed and that ego is allowed to batten on the new experience. Filled with a new inner strength, the neophyte easily forgets that this comes as a gift from outside, and is not meant simply to increase his worldly powers. He takes the credit himself, and something that should make him humble inflates his pride instead. What is gained in such cases is not merely wasted, but dangerously feeds the power instinct as well. Nor are others the only ones to get hurt; whenever something is given to serve the cause of Being and is used to achieve worldly ends, it rebounds disastrously on the user. This is why it is generally dangerous to use "initiation" exercises (which help Being to manifest itself in existence) for purely practical purposes, thus distorting them completely. This is what happens, for example, when a person treats yoga—a group of practices whose name originally meant "to yoke to Being"—like gymnastics and uses it to increase his fitness and efficiency, instead of to help him on the inner way.

Sensuous release, experience for its own sake, indolence, pride, the secular misuse of the energies of Being, and the pragmatic dilution and distortion of initiation exercises—these are the dangers that face anyone starting on the quest lightly or without proper guidance.

From Knowledge to Insight

The task that faces us all today is that of renewing ourselves by transcending objective consciousness and overcoming the dangerous limitations of the defining ego. This necessarily takes us into the realm of supernatural experience, and we must find the path that leads to—and beyond—that experience. The ways of thinking and behaving that we need here are totally different from those dictated by the defining ego, and the implications are both theoretical and practical. Thought that deals solely in opposites and dualities must yield to a vision of life rooted in supra-worldly experience, and a way of life of which insight is the keynote must grow out of that vision.

Like the term *mysticism,* the word *insight* is still an instant irritant to many "enlightened" (i.e., half-educated) Westerners—particularly when they are used to thinking in purely scientific terms. It is surely odd that a profound distrust of mysticism should often unite the loudest champions of reason, which claims to know all there is to know about reality, and the loudest champions of organized religion, which claims to know all there is to know about "higher" reality. How can this happen? Perhaps because each side feels that the mere possibility of supernatural experience, in which Being—transcending all reason, but directly felt as absolute energy, order, and unity—is revealed, threatens the seamless consistency and universal validity of the reality it has made its own.

But supernatural experience is not the whole story: also necessary is a conscious and careful process of spiritual training and development that overcomes the restrictions of dualistic thought and builds on each experience as it comes, gradually shaping the individual and making him mature in such a way that everything he experiences and does is rooted in the truth of Being, beyond all antitheses. Insight (as opposed to pragmatic knowledge) gained in this way is always the product of experiences in which Life enters us entire, because it has not been turned into a "thing"—that is, it has not been filtered through the various categories and concepts that manufacture "things," and so has not been robbed of its basic reality. Only if it is real in this sense does the relative form that it assumes in us match the absolute form embedded in our true nature.

To gain insight, we must turn inward; but merely turning from the outside world to our own inner world is not enough. The inner world, too, can be turned into a thing—as the self-analysis practiced in conventional psychology shows us. It becomes a thing, for example, whenever we "think about" ourselves or try to say exactly who and what we are. As long as consciousness remains unchanged, the difference between insight and ordinary knowledge is not a matter of looking in or out; it is a matter of turning objective into subjective consciousness.

When I once asked the great Zen teacher Daisetz T. Suzuki, "What is Eastern wisdom?" he told me: "Western knowledge looks out, Eastern wisdom looks in. But when we look in as if looking out, we turn 'in' into 'out.' " This, then, is the problem: we are constantly turning "in" into "out," i.e., turning it into a thing. But how can we stop ourselves from doing this? In other words, when we look in, how can we prevent objective consciousness from distorting our deepest experience? Surely inner experience is bound to express itself in images and concepts with objective meanings? Indeed it is—and every religion operates like this, using a consistent system of images and concepts to convey the nature and effects of a fundamental experience. But we must remember that these images and concepts are "interpreted experience" from the outset, and need to be related back to the original experience before they can be understood. Buddhism is no exception to this rule.

Just as there is no Christianity without Christ, there is no Buddhism without Gautama Buddha and without an understanding of what he suffered, experienced, and taught. And just as the mystery of Christianity is revealed only to the believer, so the mystery reveals itself in Buddhism only to a very special type of consciousness.

The starting point of Buddha's life and teaching was the question of suffering—its nature, its origin, and the possibility of finding release from it. The doctrine of the non-self, which is central to Buddhist thought, seems to follow naturally from the impermanence of everything. Similarly, human suffering seems to follow logically from an error, an illusion, a clinging to something that has no lasting reality, but dangles like a mirage before the consciousness that registers the evanescent only, and prevents us from seeing the truth. There is often a hard logic about Buddhist writings, particularly the early ones, that attracts the Western reader by its seeming clarity. But if everything the Buddhist scriptures say is so easy to understand, why was Buddha's great enlightenment needed to discover it? This question brings us to something that is often forgotten when Buddhism and other religions are being discussed: in the great religions, the truth seems to be stated in an open, accessible form, but is actually encoded. Basically, what all of them, including Buddhism, are giving us is not ordinary, instantly digestible knowledge, but an illuminated, inner, secret, insightful knowledge. One of the more sweeping and naïve distortions of Eastern wisdom is made by people who describe and interpret the supernatural meaning of Buddhist doctrine from the standpoint of ordinary, objective consciousness—and then belittle it with patronizing praise (it is "noble" and "humane") or condemn it as hybrid and misleading (it preaches "self-salvation").

The reality from which insight comes is the primal reality, with which we are always fundamentally one. We can only find this reality, however, by following a tortuous path and passing through various stages—objective consciousness taking us further from it, anguish at loss of contact with it, and final victory over that anguish—before we come back to and achieve awareness of it on the basis of a new and broader consciousness. Buddhism speaks to us of a reality that has nothing to do with the reality that our ordinary notions of life have taught us to see, the reality of everyday thought and speech. But this is not true of Buddhism only; the transcendent truth of any religious experience is obscured and distorted when we see, define, and express it with our normal, worldly understanding, or try to grasp its images and symbols in that way. This is why the great religious teachers constantly remind us that they are speaking of a truth that only the inner ear can hear and only the inner eye can see. The opening of the inner eye is a central concept in Zen. It means waking to a new and wholly different level of the self—to new strength rooted in a new consciousness. Only a new consciousness, which has nothing in common with objective consciousness, can put us in touch with the truth that really counts, and this implies a spiritual revolution. Once we have grasped this, the great adventure beckons. Are we going to meet the challenge?

Of course, a person may be happy with his old view of things, and there is nothing wrong with this—if somewhere, deep down in his feeling for life, his links with true nature have never been severed. Unconscious of his share in Being, he takes a naïvely realistic view of the world, and this need never change, unless he again experiences the unity of Being, normally concealed from him by his natural ego. But the situation changes, and changes radically, when he leaves the ego and antitheses behind, hears the call of Being, and knows that the only way to seize this new experience fully is to drop the old outlook that confines his vision to things and tangibles. If, at this point, he still claims that the divisive ego's vision and values are the only ones, he is allowing prejudice to rule his conscience and throwing away his chance of becoming an integrated, mature, and rounded human being, fully in tune with his own real nature.

Obviously, even when we have experienced Being and seen into the real heart of life, we are still free to reject all of this and opt instead for "natural" experience, objective reality, and the objective view of life's meaning. But we must know what we are doing and accept responsibility for it. Surely, having gone as far as our natural capacities will take us and come to a point where the supernatural can reveal itself to us, we should spare no effort to break the hold of the defining ego and thing-centered outlook that have given us the wonders of technology, but—as long as they dominate the scene—stop Being from coming to consciousness within us, and stop us from fulfilling ourselves in true nature.

Westerners cling to this ego and its consciousness with a stubborn pride that leaves little room for the higher consciousness in which Being is tasted through senses beyond normal sense and manifests itself in a new spirituality and a new physicality. Most of us who stand in the Western tradition still want to think that reason is preeminent, still use objective images and concepts to shore up once-for-all beliefs, and are still afraid to face up to our deepest experiences—although these are the experiences in which Being comes home to us and gives us a new and deeper knowledge. This knowledge is neither objective nor tangible, but it carries total conviction. It enables us to think about and deal with the world on a new basis and allows us to see the world's inner workings—and it breathes the truth of divine life back into our beliefs at the very point where we have fallen prey to worldly understanding with its hunger for "proofs."

The Westerner feels the anguish his native outlook has brought him, but he also feels the futility of trying to relieve it by the very means that have caused it. If the easy way out—running from himself into apathy, conformity, and resignation—is no longer enough, he must listen to the voice of his innermost nature, which can never be objectively grasped. This, too, is a part of Zen's message. If we approach it with open, questing minds, we may find that, far from being merely Eastern, it is actually saying, in its own way, something that the great thinkers of the West have also known and taught, and which has always been the creative, renewing wellspring of life. When a person hears the inescapable, unmistakable call of his true nature, there can no longer be any question of not answering it. When he has an experience in which the Absolute touches and summons him, and fails to respond, he is missing the way he was meant to follow, and will pay the price for doing so.

Zen's Answer

Woe to this degenerate age
Of consummate unbelief!
Empty of virtue, people
Are scarcely now to be bettered.
Too long have they been
By holiness deserted,
And wrong thinking
Has eaten deep into them.
Since truth is so weak,
The devil rules them,
And evildoers and enemies of truth
Are not few in number.
Now it angers them that they too,
Powerless to destroy or rend it in pieces,
Must listen face-to-face to the teaching
Of him who is come.

—SHODOKA

("The Song of the Experience of Truth,"
by Master Yoka, c. 800.)

The Sublime
Message of Zen

Everyone, in His True Nature, Is Buddha

Deep in their true nature, people are Buddha,
As water is ice. And as without water
There is no ice, so without Buddha
There is no one.
Woe to those who seek afar off
And know not what is close at hand!
They are like people standing in water
And shouting for water nonetheless.
Born noble and rich beyond counting,
They wander their way as if poor, wretched
And unsolaced.

—SONG OF THE ZEN
MASTER HAKUIN

On my travels in Japan, I once met a Christian missionary who had worked in a small village, way out in the country, for eighteen years. He had had his share of problems, but had made the occasional genuine conversion. "The only thing," he said, "is that, when their time comes, these people die as Japanese and not as Christians." I asked him what he meant, and he explained: "When they come into the world, it's as if they put only one foot on this shore, and never forget that they really belong on the other. And so 'dying' is simply a question of pulling back the foot that they've put in this life—they do it naturally, cheerfully, and without a trace of fear."

This is the old Oriental feeling about life. But must it be Oriental only? Surely we should be able to have it, as well? Or do we regard it as the kind of primitive belief that only a childish and undeveloped mind can come up with? If we do, we are responding only to that part of the fundamental insight which has found its way into a rational system of thought—and lost its truth in the process.

In practice, our readiness to accept the truth of human experience and wisdom still usually stops at the point where we can no longer "classify" what we hear. This is our Western reluctance to go beyond objective facts, that is, facts that are not colored by personal experience—although it is only beyond these facts that transcendent reality reveals itself and can be "tasted." Even when it has not explicitly entered our consciousness, however, the reality of Being still lives in our true nature, in what we fundamentally are. For Buddhists, this true nature is Buddha-nature; thus all of us, deep within ourselves, are Buddha. But we are not aware of this—although all our "vague longings" are unconsciously expressing the secret power of this true nature, drawing us into itself.

"Surely," I once asked D. T. Suzuki, "a person looking for the truth is like a fish looking for water?" "Yes," the old teacher answered, "but even more like water looking for water!" This sums it all up, humanity's problem and Zen's answer—which also holds true for us in the West! There is another Oriental saying: "The drop of water may know that

48

the ocean contains it—but does it also know that it contains the ocean?"

We often say that someone is "trying to find himself." But no one can ever find himself unless the self that seeks is the same as the self that is sought. If this is true, and if the self that is found is the same as the self that finds it, then who seeks and who is sought? We are touching here on an ultimate mystery. A mystery for whom? Possibly only for people whose consciousness is solely of the classifying and dissecting type. It is only by overcoming this consciousness that we can live the mystery as Life become conscious of itself—Life, which we ourselves are.

The Experience of Being

Zen is the doctrine of Being, of the experience of Being and of life rooted in Being. This doctrine is not a philosophical theory of being, and has nothing to do with metaphysical inquiry, but expresses an inner *experience*—the experience of Being, which we ourselves *are,* in our true nature. This experience is the consequence, content, and medium of a certain *consciousness;* indeed, it is itself the consciousness in which Life achieves awareness of itself in human beings.

When we experience our true nature, we experience Being, since our true nature is the mode in which Being is present within us. Thus, Zen does not offer us a supernatural revelation or ask us, who live in the ego and its world, to believe in an otherworldly redeemer. Zen expresses a supernatural experience and shows us an otherworldly something in which we *are* redeemed, and in which, in a certain sense, we have never been anything else. Of course, when this experience suddenly comes to a normal person leading a normal life, it may seem like a supernatural revelation. In Buddhism, this supra-worldly something is known as Buddha-nature. It is the light within us, and when we wake to it and see that it is there, it illuminates us and changes us utterly.

To experience Being for the first time is always to experience a promise as well—the promise that we can break through from what we *have* (the worldly ego's province) to what we *are* (the supra-worldly come to consciousness in our true nature). In this case, "knowing" what we are does not mean "having" it as an "object" of consciousness; it means experiencing in the self what the self truly is.

Zen is experience and experience only: experience sought, experience found, experience affirmed, experience heeded, experience made fruitful, experience borne witness to. And so Zen knowledge is never knowledge *of* something *(savoir),* but direct personal knowing *(connaissance),* and Zen itself vanishes the moment this personal knowing is reduced to objective knowledge. Entangled in the ego and befogged by the so-called facts conjured up before us by objective consciousness, we have no contact with this experience and live out our lives in error and anguish, until what we *are* bursts into what we merely *have,* and everything is suddenly flooded with light and instantly, totally *is.* It is at this moment that the divine arrow at last hits its mark, wounding us with a great longing and inexorably drawing us home. Following its pull, we become seekers of the way, and "not knowing the way, we move forward on the way, with hands outstretched, with hands outstretched. . . ."[1] And then we meet someone who senses at once that we are looking for the way and in whom we recognize ourselves as seekers, someone who happens to cross our path at that very moment—or perhaps only the master in ourselves. If we choose to follow him, the great light may suddenly shine out in us. Taking fire and rising, we find the *way* stretching before us, and for the first time it is the great *way to total change*—change that is both purpose and never-ending process.

But what exactly is this watershed experience, this experience that underlies the whole of Zen and on which the whole of Zen centers, this experience that Zen exercises pre-

1. Ancient Indian saying.

pare us for, and that takes on form in other exercises that remake us, this experience that is expressed in conflict, creativity, and love? This question will not go away, and we have to answer it anew whenever our understanding and insight deepen. To have the Zen experience is to experience our true nature and Being coming to consciousness within it. It is to experience Being in and through our true nature. It is to experience Being as what we are, beyond all the concepts and images of "having." It is to experience Being as a universal brotherhood in which we all share and that gives us the key to every language and religion—allowing us to see one another as we are, in the same fullness, light, and love.

We cannot experience Being in the way that we experience a tree, a thing, another person—as objects distinct and apart from ourselves. Being and true nature can be sensed only as an indwelling presence. But how can we experience this presence without its becoming an "object" of consciousness—since all experience depends on consciousness? Obviously, we are talking of a special type of experience and of a wholly new type of consciousness. It is only in this new consciousness that Life can become an inner presence, and only in this experience that Life—which we ourselves are—can fulfill itself by becoming what it truly is. "Life cannot be fulfilled unless it return to its plain source, in which life is Being, which the soul receives when it dies to itself, so that we may live in that life in which life is Being," wrote Meister Eckhart. This, then, is the Zen experience—the experience of Life as Being, before the two have been estranged by the consciousness that sorts the unity of "being" into the multiplicity of "having." This consciousness is itself a natural part of being human, and so we cannot rid ourselves of it; but if we are entirely ruled by it, the illusions of possession and attachment ensnare us and prevent us from making the breakthrough.

The consciousness that separates us from the animals also separates us from God—when it claims to be absolute. Prevented by it from seeing the truth ourselves, we immediately denounce as "mad" anyone who sees and behaves in a wholly new manner after his first encounter with Being—until he returns to what we wrongly regard as normalcy or finds Being *in* having, and successfully preserves its inner presence in his everyday existence. To have the Zen experience is thus to wake from the illusion that objective, dualistic consciousness is the only one that counts, and to shed both its deadening systems and the habit of thinking in things and antitheses—not only in sorting and dealing with the world, but in dealing with and searching for the living truth. To break the illusion is to break the spell of objective thought, and thus the hold of dualism. The essential step on the path to this freedom is taken by silencing discursive thought and listening to the voice that speaks in and out of the silence that follows when dualistic thinking has been left behind.

The Experience of Being and Dualism

> *Stubbornly to seek the truth's deepest meaning*
> *Is to wear yourself out in idle cogitation.*
> *Put your thinking to silence—*
> *That is what matters!*
> *Do not linger in thought*
> *Upon antitheses;*
> *To chase after and seek them—*
> *Beware of so doing!*
> *For one breath of antithesis*
> *Hands your spirit over to confusion.*

—From the Shin Jin Mei (Seal of Belief)
  by the Third Patriarch, Sosan

Zen is the doctrine of Being transcending all antitheses, Being in which there is no before and after, no here and there, no this and that, no Peter and Paul. This is the problem Zen sets the thinker—particularly the Westerner, who naturally thinks in antitheses, and the Christian believer, who naturally feels that he cannot survive without dualism. A Christian priest once said to me, "You can write what you like—as long as you keep dualism." Why did he say that? Because, for him, dropping dualism meant accepting "monism," and that ultimately meant denying the distance between human beings and God, fusing the two—and seriously shaking one of the main pillars of Christian belief. But is this really what it means? It is—if we take the unity of nonobjective experience, reinterpret it in objective terms, and equate it with identity. If we do this, we are turning non-dualism into an objective "one," in which all human beings are one—and in which God and mankind are also one. This "one" is perceived as "something," in which all distinctions are resolved and everything becomes identical—certainly a blasphemous notion when applied to the man/God relationship.

If we go on and attribute this blasphemy to Zen, we are missing Zen's decisive message, and will continue to miss it until we can break the hold of objective consciousness. The experience of Being is the experience of opposites that coincide. The objective, dualistic view of reality that objective consciousness gives us is an illusion, and when it falls away, Being reveals itself to us as fullness, order, and unity transcending all antitheses. In Zen, all of this is experienced, tasted, sensed in a way that leaves no room for doubt. To describe it is not to state a theory of being, but to recount a deeply personal experience, one in which we experience our true nature as one of this unity's modes, and experience this unity in our true nature's language. Every antithesis between person and thing, between "I" and "you"—and thus between the self and God—is superseded and resolved when we experience this unity, in which there is no "two." Afterward, although we still live in the dualistic ego and "see" through its dualistic consciousness, dualism itself is lifted onto a higher plane. The image of God fashioned by the old consciousness, which had turned God into an external "thing," recedes, and the very fact of having experienced divine unity—and ourselves as a part of that unity—as the ultimate reality makes us feel the contrast between ourselves and God, the All-One, all the more keenly once we have left that unity behind and are back in the ego; but we also have a powerful sense of being intimately connected with God in a way that confining Him within a mere external image makes impossible. God now lies beyond imaginings and concepts. Doubt, which pertains to ego-vision only, no longer has anything to fasten on, and unity experienced *within* the incomprehensible generates the true belief that doubt—which is sparked only *by* the incomprehensible—cannot touch.

This kind of belief is only possessed a priori by people who, living in the ego, have retained a basic contact with unity. But unity is lost from view as objective consciousness tightens its grip—and belief goes with it. The Zen experience holds the answer here; it can lead all those who have irrevocably lost their old beliefs to true belief—including true Christian belief. (Obviously, Buddhists are not the only ones who can have this experience.)

The basic realization is always the same—that the stream of life divides in two when it hits the ego-centered consciousness; its pure light is refracted by the ego's prism and split into antitheses. Once this happens and the primal life-consciousness divides into a self/object consciousness, life necessarily presents itself in dualisms: before/after, here/there, transient/permanent, relative/absolute, spirit/matter, etc. A person who identifies entirely with this ego naturally shrinks from anything that threatens his individual permanence. And he naturally thinks of Being—experienced as the antithesis of contingent, perishable, here-and-now existence and as a challenge to the ego's stability and logic—as absolute, everlasting, and unlimited. But this conception of the Absolute is rooted in the ego's thinking and is valid only from the ego's standpoint. It imposes the basic pattern of egocentric thought on the Absolute and projects it outside the individual, turning it, like anything else experienced and thought, into a "thing," an object of consciousness. Here again, the static ego and its consciousness interpose and cut us off from the truth.

When we identify with the defining ego and accept the reality it gives us as an object of consciousness, we are robbed of divine reality, which is never an object of consciousness and can never be represented objectively. And so we fall into doubt, always a sign that true unity—the unity that becomes an inner presence in satori—has been lost.

What makes us sacrifice something we have experienced in that unity, with total, unquestioning clarity, to a vision of reality that is rooted in the defining, divisive ego? Only our inability to shake off that ego's spell. What, when we have experienced satori, makes us bow to the stubborn misconceptions of people who have either never experienced it or have lacked the courage to follow it up? Only the fear that comes from confusing what we have actually experienced ourselves with what others mistakenly believe we have experienced. If, having had the mystical experience of unity, we look back on it objectively, mistake it for everlasting sameness, and run from it in horror, then we have simply failed to understand the grace we have received. We are setting the reality we imagine, a reality engendered by reason and subject to its laws, above the reality we experience.

Of course, even when we have experienced the unity that transcends all antitheses, we remain tied to the old ego with its antithetical thought patterns. But when Being enters us, everything—even the things we see objectively through the old ego—is transfigured. This is because we can now see antitheses—including the man/God antithesis—as the way in which ultimate unity is reflected in the ego. We can also experience for ourselves how the gap between us and the objectively "other" disappears when we encounter a "you" in whom absolute *unity* is present and active. When God is truly, intimately present to a person, the sense of oneness with God that he has experienced in his true nature will persist—even when his ego insists that God is infinitely far away. Neither the objective ego nor belief that insists on an absolute distance can bridge the gap between God and mankind—but the Zen experience can.

The Doctrine of Not-Two

Believing is not-two.
Not-two is believing
In that which cannot be uttered.
Are not
Past and future
An everlasting now?

—From the Shin Jin Mei

Speaking of the "One" undoubtedly causes serious misunderstandings—and this is why Zen speaks of the "not-two" instead.

When it says "not-two," it is saying that the One that
it means is not "something" different from "not-one." Thus,
if we try to describe the Being experienced in satori by saying
that Zen is the doctrine of the One, and that this One is
something that transcends all antitheses, we are missing the
real point of Zen—because Being cannot be described.

The first glorious experience of a non-dualistic absolute
beyond time and space can lead to another misunderstanding:
the conviction that this is in itself the experience of truth
transcending antitheses. This is not so. It is true that the first
experience of Being beyond space and time, which shatters
the spell of ego-based reality, always has a bright, happy,
"heavenly" feeling. But transcendence experienced as otherworldly brightness is followed at once by transcendence experienced as darkness—as if hell showed its face only to those
who had seen heaven and only the experience of absolute
good could steel them to encounter absolute evil. The One
that really transcends antitheses is revealed only in the experience of Light beyond light and darkness—which follows the
experience of darkness. When we first experience Being, we
experience the absence of antitheses, but we immediately contrast this experience with ego-reality, which is ruled by antitheses, thus showing that the defining, divisive consciousness

is still with us. And so we fall short of ultimate knowledge, which stays out of reach while we remain rooted in the old consciousness or, having overcome it briefly, relapse and cling to it again as the only one that counts. Absence of antitheses, perceived through this consciousness, is still not transcendence of antitheses, which comes in the real Zen experience: satori.

The Being that is talked about in Zen does not reveal itself to us until we realize that non-antithetical and antithetical reality are fundamentally one—or, to put it more accurately, not-two. But this is surely as far as thought can take us? Certainly, and this is precisely the point: the truly supra-antithetical cannot come to inner consciousness until thinking stops, is suspended, or is neutralized. In other words, when Zen speaks of not-two, it is not asking us to follow a chain of reasoning that leads by logical steps to a logically impossible conclusion; it is speaking of an experience that we can have as human beings, but that lies beyond the reach of logic.

The ultimate negation of dualism is precisely what satori is not. What we experience in satori is the reconciliation of non-dualistic and dualistic thought—and this reconciliation comes when satori itself makes us see that the ego, with its divisive consciousness and its system of antitheses, is not merely disruptive of unity, but is actually also the medium through which ultimate unity reveals itself inwardly for the first time. We come to see that dualism is in fact the mode in which Being, which transcends it utterly, must manifest itself to us as long as we identify with the ego and its consciousness. It is only clinging to dualism that is fatal. In fact, anyone who knows anything about satori sees the defining ego's worldview as a divine gift to humanity, for it is only against the background of this worldview that redemptive Being and redeemed existence come to consciousness.

The doctrine of the One—which is not *the* One because it is not something, but not-two—is central to Zen. Zen repeatedly tells us that this true One has not been properly revealed to us as long as we continue to see it as the opposite of something else that is *not* the One. This means that we can never ask "What is it?" since the question alone shows that we are on the wrong track. If we see it as the "supra-antithetical," the "supra-worldly," "Being," or "void" in opposition to the antithetical, the worldly, existence, or plenitude—or even contrast it mentally with these—not-two at once disappears. We are forced to use words in referring to it, but the moment we use a word and thus define something, misunderstanding threatens. We always start by contrasting our own experience of non-antithesis with such everyday antitheses as many/few, poor/rich, strong/weak, light/dark, good/evil, something/ nothing—and then try to overcome this obvious inconsistency by calling it "the void." Immediately, however—and although we are applying it to an experience beyond anti- theses—the word *void* itself acquires antithetical significance. Zen is always alive to this fatal property of words, and this is why it treats them with caution.

The void that we define as void—and we can do so only by contrasting it with the non-void—is still not the true Void. The true Void does not come to inner consciousness until this antithesis, too, has been eliminated. When we then use the word *void* to denote the void revealed to us in our true nature, we mean something entirely different, and so we shift into upper case—Void—to make the distinction. This, of course, is confusing and a constant source of misunderstandings of the kind we face when Meister Eckhart speaks of "God," and we are left wondering whether he means the Godhead, "which is as far above God as the heaven is above the earth" (i.e., the Godhead that transcends all antitheses, including the ego/ God antithesis), or the God who "passes out of being when the ego passes out of being." Similarly, when we read Zen texts, we must always try hard to work out what they are really saying. As used in Zen texts, however, the term *void* nearly always means Void.

What is true of Void is also true of Love beyond love and hate, Justice beyond justice and injustice, Life beyond life and death, Being beyond being and nonbeing, Form beyond form and formlessness, Light beyond light and darkness, and so on. But Void, Love, Justice, Being, Form, and Light reveal themselves to us in the Zen sense only when objective, antithetical consciousness has been wholly replaced by subjective consciousness.

There is, of course, another love beyond love and hate, namely "Christian" love, which is bestowed, regardless of liking or disliking, on enemies no less than friends. But although it transcends these antitheses, this love is still itself the antithesis of a condition in which we are torn between love and non-love. The Love that really lies beyond antitheses is at the heart of non-love no less than love—and also at the heart of fluctuation between the two. Only that which speaks from this Love is not-two, or Being, to which we can no longer attach the definite article (*the* One), since it is not a definite thing, but Being—the inexpressible beginning and end, the alpha and omega, the *true nature* of all things.

Whenever Being "emerges" as an inner presence, it wears a different face—revealing itself as love, void, life, truth, reality, depending on the particular antithesis from which the individual starts. This is the ultimate mystery, and it comes to us only in the void and remains with us only in silence. But it is always *the same not-two* that is revealed—*the same One* that is sensed in all of life's manifestations by those who experience it. Basically, there is nothing that can be said about it, and yet people are constantly asking what they are to "understand" by it—only to realize at last that silence is the final answer to their question.

Then Vimalakirti also turned to all the assembled bodhisattvas and asked: "My lords, how may a bodhisattva enter the realm of not-two?"

In the assembly of the bodhisattvas, there was one Dharmesvara, who began: "My lords, coming into being and ceasing to be are two—but things have never really come into being and so cannot cease to be. To penetrate the truth of this law of not-coming-into-being is to enter the realm of not-two."

The Bodhisattva Gunagupta said: " 'I' and 'mine' are two. Because there is an 'I,' there is also a 'mine.' If there were no 'I,' there would be no 'mine,' either. To realize this is to enter the realm of not-two."

The Bodhisattva Gunasiras said: "Purity and impurity are two; whoever grasps the true nature of impurity sees that neither purity nor impurity exists—and so follows the purity of nirvana. To realize this is to enter the realm of not-two."

The Bodhisattva Sunetra said: "Form and formlessness are two. To discern formlessness in form is to enter the oneness of things without clinging to formlessness. To realize this is to enter the realm of not-two."

The Bodhisattva Pusya said: "Good and not-good are two. To think neither good nor not-good is to arrive at nondiscrimination and to recognize the truth. To realize this is to enter the realm of not-two."

The Bodhisattva Simha said: "Sin and virtue are two. To understand the nature of sin completely is also to understand that it does not differ from virtue. To realize this is to enter the realm of not-two."

The Bodhisattva Narayana spoke as follows: "Worldliness and supra-worldliness are two. To see that the nature of worldliness is futility is to discover the nature of supra-worldliness, in which there is neither entering nor leaving, neither overflowing nor dispersal. To realize this is to enter the realm of not-two."

The Bodhisattva Sadhumati said: "Samsara [the cycle of rebirth] and nirvana are two. To understand the nature of samsara is to know that there is neither samsara nor attachment nor liberation nor extinction. To realize this is to enter the realm of not-two."

The Bodhisattva Pratyaksa said: "Annihilation and non-annihilation are two. If, in their true natures, all things are neither destroyed nor not-destroyed, there is no form of destruction, and if there is no form of destruction, this is the void—and the void has the form of neither destruction nor nondestruction. To attain this sphere of truth is to enter the realm of not-two."

The Bodhisattva Vidyuddeva said: "Knowing and not-knowing [enlightenment and error] are two. The true nature of not-knowing, however, is knowing. Knowing cannot be grasped, since it lies beyond all distinctions. To persist in this belief and be free of the thought of duality is to enter the realm of not-two."

The Bodhisattva Punyaksetra said: "Virtuous and sinful conduct, and conduct that is neither sinful nor virtuous, are two. In itself, the nature of these three types of conduct is empty; if it is empty, there is ultimately neither virtuous nor sinful nor indifferent conduct. To realize this is to enter the realm of not-two."

The Bodhisattva Puspavyuha said: "Duality arises from the ego; a person who understands the true nature of the ego is not ruled by dualistic thought; a person who clings to neither of these opposites has neither a subject nor an object of consciousness, and enters the realm of not-two."

The Bodhisattva Srigarbha said: "Attachment and non-attachment to things are two; if there is no attachment to things, things are neither taken nor relinquished. To realize this is to enter the realm of not-two."

The Bodhisattva Ratnamudrahasta said: "Longing for the world and longing for nirvana are two; if a person does not long for nirvana and is not weary of the world, then duality ceases. Why? Because if there is attachment, there is also liberation—but if there is no attachment to start with, there can surely be no point in longing for release. If there is neither attachment nor release, then there is no joy [in nirvana] and no weariness [of the world]. To realize this is to enter the realm of not-two."

The Bodhisattva Manicudaraja answered: "Honesty and dishonesty are two. The person who is truly honest makes no distinction between honesty and dishonesty. To be free of this duality is to enter the realm of not-two."

The Bodhisattva Satyapriha said: "Reality and non-reality are two. When reality is understood, it is not seen—and how much more is non-reality not seen. Why is this? Reality cannot be seen with the eye of the body, but only with the eye of wisdom—and in the eye of wisdom there is no seeing which is the opposite of not-seeing. To realize this is to enter the realm of not-two."

When all the bodhisattvas had spoken their minds in this fashion, they asked Manjusri: "What does it mean when a bodhisattva enters the realm of not-two?" Manjusri answered: "My view *is that nothing can be said or explained, described or understood in this matter, and that the whole question cannot even be discussed. To realize this is to enter the realm of not-two."*

Then Manjusri said to Vimalakirti: "Each of us has now had his say—and I would ask you, Lord, also to tell us your opinion as to how a bodhisattva enters the realm of not-two."

> *Vimalakirti entered the circle,*
> knelt—and said nothing.
> *This is known as "the thunderous silence of Vimalakirti."*

And they took their answer from this mighty silence.[2]

How many of us know how to listen properly—to listen so that silence speaks? The wisdom of the East is born of silence, and so is the wisdom of Zen. Zen teaches us how to listen to and hear the silence of Being, which—amid all the noises of the world—is calling us into the truth.

> *There is no grasping the nature of true nature*
> *And no casting it aside.*
> *Only so can the center*
> *Of the unattainable*
> *Be attained.*
> *It is silent when it speaks*
> *And speaks when it is silent.*
> *Wide open stands the mighty door*
> *Of the giver*
> *Truth.*
>
> —SHODOKA

2. Adapted from the ninth chapter of the Vimalakirti Sutra.

Non-attachment to "Being"

Every two depends upon the One
But with this alone you must not rest content.
Do not chase Being, the ever-active,
And do not stop at non-Being, the empty.
When you find the One
And are freed into serenity,
All of this will fall
Effortlessly from you.
If, wanting motion to be stilled,
You return to this one thing, hoping to find stillness,
You only drive stillness
Further into movement.
For how can you grasp the One
While you still hesitate
Between One and Other?
If you do not understand
The One,
You lose even what the two
Has brought you.
Being recedes
When you pursue it;
Nothingness turns its back
When you run after it.
A thousand words and
A thousand thoughts
Take you only further from it.
Thought seizes nothing
But shells without substance.
If thought guides you,
Even for a moment,
You lose yourself
In the void of the not-something
Whose mutability and transience
Are born entirely of your error.

—from SHIN JIN MEI

When a person has gone as far as his natural strength and wisdom can take him, and finds himself able to accept death, meaninglessness, and absolute loneliness, forgetting the terror and despair they once caused him, he is doing something that his ego alone cannot do. It is at this very moment that he may receive the grace of that experience in which he senses the strength, meaning, and unity of Being, and suddenly feels himself redeemed and liberated into new life. His joy is indescribable. Fear, despair, and desolation vanish. He feels filled with power, flooded with light, utterly sheltered, and totally at peace. Radiantly, he tastes the power that has freed him into himself. Small wonder that, having sought the ultimate experience, he believes that he has found it at last—but the blow soon falls and he finds that he is wrong.

The happiness fades, and so does the strength that made him feel immortal, the meaning that carried him far beyond unmeaning, and the love that filled his solitude. All of this fades, and he feels the world's threatening presence more sharply than before. The very experience that seemed to free him from anguish forever now plunges him into the anguish of an even deeper despair. For now, having actually tasted what he had only believed in, hoped for, and dimly sensed before—limitless, absolute, supra-worldly Being—he is fully aware for the first time how relative, restricted, and narrow the world really is. Now that he has glimpsed the great light, the darkness seems even darker. A tormented exile from a lost paradise, he wants only to find once again the unutterably wonderful thing he has experienced, and, having found it, to dwell in it forever. How natural this longing is—but how clearly it shows that dualism still clings to him and that his experience of Being is still not satori, the experience promised in Zen. His own experience has registered as "something" immeasurably different from the world to which he has returned—and he wants to have it again and possess it forever. But this is chasing a mirage, for, by trying to *have* the experience again, he actually drives it away, because there is nothing to "have." Transformation in Being is what it is all about.

Even plumbing the depths of our own soul may do us no good, if a pleasant sensation of emptiness is all we get out of it.

"When you find yourself plunged in reverie so delightful that you would choose to remain in it forever, tear yourself free," said Meister Eckhart, "and seize on the task next to hand, for these are melting sensations and nothing else!" Melting sensations! And this is also the temptation permanently involved in looking for release through artificial means. A drug-induced "high" merely cries out to be repeated and rarely engenders the new sense of moral purpose that every true experience of Being brings with it—the stern inner call to self-transformation and unremitting practice—so that we can at last become permanently anchored in what we have experienced. Lacking this power to transform and mold conscience, the drug experience is an illicit experience. If it is repeated and becomes addictive, it ushers in a process of regression that actually bars the path to higher development.

A person called to the *way* always finds the world he lives in as a "natural human being" too narrow, but the only way of overcoming this world is to push boldly on and grow beyond it. We cannot shake off the burden of world-being by turning our backs on the world and trying to steal away from it, but only by facing up to it and smashing straight through to its inner immensities. To do this, however, we need another kind of experience, an experience we can have only if, having once known supra-worldly unity, we find it again in and with the world. We *understand* only if, in this experience, we see what divides us from unity, and if we succeed in bearing witness through this dividing element.

The Opening of the Inner Eye

If we use the words *Being, Void,* and *not-two* in an effort to understand Zen, and if we think of these ideas as something definite, the great danger is always that the new consciousness, which understands, may be basically the same as the old one, which prevented us from understanding. Ultimately, we are dealing with something that cannot be understood, and yet there always seem to be ways of hinting at it that can themselves be understood. Any attempt to provide a comprehensible account of Zen—including the present one—puts everything at risk; it invariably classifies something that cannot be classified, or at least connects it with a system of thought, even if that system is a broadened one.

The most that thought, pushed to its furthest limits, can give us is the rind of a fruit—the rind we must crush to reach the fruit itself. And so we must accept what is so hard to accept: that a higher reality cannot emerge in satori as long as our consciousness remains unchanged, but only when the old consciousness has been destroyed and a new one forged. And since consciousness determines the subjective self, we can also say that enlightenment depends upon the subject's having a new stance—or, more accurately, that it coincides with our birth as a new subject.

It is a common mistake to assume that "enlightenment" means the dawning of a new light that allows us to see something new, while we ourselves remain the same. Of course, this can happen too—when suddenly we see a problem, thing, or person in a new light and all our uncertainties are instantly dispelled, or when we unexpectedly see something we had failed to see only a moment before. This experience—when a whole series of seemingly unconnected elements suddenly falls into place and forms a pattern—can be a powerful one. And people can indeed be enlightened concerning the way in which everything fits together; they suddenly have a new worldview, giving them a new security and firing them with new energy. But this has nothing whatsoever to do with the enlightenment, the *awakening,* that is central to Zen. In Zen, it is less a matter of the old eye's showing us a new world than of a new eye's remaking the old world for us. This new eye is not simply the old one enlightened. Enlightenment does not mean that the ice around us melts, but that our own substance is changed; it means that we transform both ourselves and our way of seeing and, becoming new, see new things in a new way.

However powerful it may be, the experience of Being as something "utterly different" is still not enlightenment, still not awakening, still not the opening of the inner eye—still not satori. However great our joy may be when we experience Being as something beyond all objective antitheses, this experience is merely a foretaste of the experience of ultimate truth. *Dissolution of the ego in true nature* is only the first step, and leads to nothing unless it is followed by the second: *true nature's unfolding in the ego.* The inner eye, as Zen understands it, opens only when the experience of Being reveals unity to us in and with the world, showing us that the world is both the barrier that divides us from Being *and* the medium through which Being, the world's hidden true nature, manifests itself and forces its way toward the light.

When a person "wakes," Being not only becomes an inner presence, but the cause that obscured it, the "root of evil," is seen *from within.* The opening of the inner eye is also—and chiefly—the unmasking of the ego.

> *Seeking the builder of this dwelling,*
> *I vainly passed through the cycle*
> *Of many births—*
> *Births, like all births, freighted with sorrow.*
> *But now, builder of the tent, you are known*
> *And shall build it no more.*
> *Your rafters are broken,*
> *Your cross-ties all shattered.*
> *Free of all bonds, redeemed,*
> *The spirit has come, where all desires cease.*

This hymn is attributed to Buddha, who is said to have composed it at the time of his enlightenment. D. T. Suzuki glosses it like this: "The monster, the house-builder, the constructor of the prison-house, being known, being seen, being caught, ceases at last to weave his entrapping network around Buddha."[3]

This realization comes in satori as a shattering personal experience, and is much more than an abstract grasping of the fact that the defining ego and its consciousness conceal Being from us, in that recognition of the ego *experienced* in satori actually breaks its hold on us. This is not to say that we no longer have to *live* under the restrictions and conditions imposed on us by the ego once we have had this experience, but we *exist* from another source. We are no longer enslaved by the ego and its way of seeing, and no longer at the mercy of the anguish it causes.

At the same time, the unmasking of the ego as the great sinner and separator, and liberation from it, is only one side of the knowledge that comes in satori.

The inner eye looks in two directions. It sees both the world-self and the true self, and once it opens, we see the world-self not only as a constant threat to Being's inner presence, but also as the medium through which Being reveals itself in here-and-now existence. We know that the ego, with its static concepts and its fixed images and attitudes, is constantly barring the path to true life, but we also know that Being manifests itself only in the anguish caused us by the ego's concealment of it and the ego's limitations. Being transcends all antitheses, but it can come to consciousness only against the background of something that contradicts it—and static ego-reality serves a positive function by providing that background. The opening of the inner eye, looking in two directions, lets us see that the dualistic world renders us one inestimable service in that it manifests the One to us in this very dualism, and constantly prepares us for the One in the anguish caused us by this same dualism. And so we really "see" only if we experience Being without trying to hang on to it, if we recognize it without seeing it as "something," if we

3. D. T. Suzuki, *Mysticism: Christian and Buddhist* (Westport, Conn.: Greenwood Press, 1976).

surrender to it without losing ourselves in it, if we can go back to the world no longer the same but transformed, preserving the undiminished experience within us and henceforth able to see and interpret the world only in terms of Being. Born to ourselves from our true nature, we live as changed beings in a world of change. As D. T. Suzuki explains, it is the relative, empirical ego that has been unmasked, and the spirit freed of that ego's restrictions is the absolute ego. "Enlightenment consists in seeing into the meaning of life as the interplay of the relative ego with the absolute ego. In other words, enlightenment is seeing the absolute ego as reflected in the relative ego and acting through it. Or we may express the idea in this way: the absolute ego creates the relative ego in order to see itself reflected in it, that is, in the relative ego. The absolute ego, as long as it remains absolute, has no means whereby to assert itself, to manifest itself, to work out all its possibilities. It requires a relative ego to execute its biddings."[4]

Recognition of the right relationship between Being and existence, between the reality of the absolute ego and the objective world of the empirical ego, lies at the heart of enlightenment; thus enlightenment itself is not merely a redeeming vision, but makes positive demands on us. It is true that the objective world has become "transparent" once and for all, allowing Being to show through—but the real task now is to bring Being into everything we see and do, to make existence fully real in terms of Being. It is this new sense of responsibility toward a new world, and not merely the breaking of the old one's spell, that really makes the Zen experience satori.

If ultimate unity genuinely has us in its grip, we have a sense of being deeply at one with the world and all humanity, connected with them in the true nature that we share; and we also share a common destiny: that of becoming what we are in our true natures. What we feel for one another expresses what our true nature makes us, what we aspire to be and what

4. Ibid.

we should be: brothers and sisters in Being, born to go through life together and to help one another toward awareness of what we really are, transforming ourselves in the process, so that the Absolute can shine through the form we wear in this contingent world. This is where compassion and companionship really begin, in the urge to help others to tear from their eyes the veil of the ego, the ego that sees antitheses only and deludes us into thinking that these antitheses are the true reality. D. T. Suzuki reminds us that enlightenment is not fleeing from the world and sitting cross-legged on a mountaintop, calmly watching while people bomb other people down below; there are more tears to it than we like to think.[5]

And so satori is not blissfully dissolving in All/One/Being; it means constantly seeing, creating, and bearing witness to Being in existence, to the true self in the ego, to the Absolute in the relative, to the divine in the world.

In satori, the world is suddenly given to us afresh, with a new meaning and a new radiance, as promise and as obligation. The fields are still green, but the green is a deeper green. Humanity is still human, but human in a higher sense and called to a new life. Is there anything here to set Zen at odds with Christian thought?

What Zen Looks Like in Practice

The moon pours light
Across the stream abundantly.
The pines breathe softly.
Who is leading this sacred evening
Toward everlasting night?
Deep in his heart he wears the seal,
The flawless pearl of Buddha-nature.

5. D. T. Suzuki, *Introduction to Zen Buddhism* (New York: Grove Press, 1964).

Whenever a person has the Zen experience, life becomes Life, penetrates the essence of his human life, and becomes that essence. Within it, he continues to live his physical life in the here-and-now, like everyone else, but he himself is different, lives his life differently, and lives it with a different purpose.

"To be ordinary is Zen, and to be contrary is not Zen; your daily life, however much you have Zen, is not to deviate from that of your neighbors. If there is any deviation, it must be in your inner life." But daily life is now rooted in Life become conscious of itself. "This is not, however, that dark consciousness of the brute or child which is waiting for development and clarification. It is, on the contrary, that form of consciousness which we can attain only after years of hard seeking and hard thinking."[6] When his inner eye has been opened, a person continues to live normally in the here-and-now, but transcendence enters the here-and-now. Having awakened to Being, he lives from his true nature, as a self poised between past and future, in an everlasting now. And because he lives in this everlasting now, space and time are transformed. He suffers like anyone else, but somewhere he suffers as if he did not suffer, and—whatever pain the world causes him—he never loses the radiant good humor that comes from deep within. So what does Zen look like in practice?

Laughter, perhaps—uncontrollable laughter, exploding all the certainties of a moment back. Anger, perhaps—erupting selfless and uncaused. Movement as natural and flowing as the flight of a bird winging effortlessly higher. Action rapid and precise: essentials only—nothing else! Fetch water when there's a fire, and do that only. Eat when you're hungry, and do that only. Sleep when you sleep, and do that only. Write when you write, and do that only. Everything conscious, alive, and direct, with never a breath between thinking and doing. No holding back, just letting life flow

6. Both quotations are from D. T. Suzuki, *Living by Zen,* ed. Christmas Humphreys (New York: S. Weiser, 1976).

from the center—as free and light as a wingbeat, as true as an arrow flying to its mark, as weightless as a dance step, as devastating as a sword blow, as precise as a sculptor's chisel, as liberating as the breath of spring, and always suffused with love. No clinging, no cleaving to anything. Stillness in the very heart of tumult. Every moment as fresh as dew, and as deep as a well reflecting the stars and all eternity with them. Sharing all the world's sufferings and never questioning the role we have to play in it. Merciless to ourselves and unsparing of others—as the love that bears witness to a higher law commands us. And always the strong serenity that a kind of dying has taught us, the clarity and cheerfulness that come of sensing a meaning that embraces unmeaning, and the happiness that comes of feeling safe, whatever the world may inflict on us.

> *Walking is Zen,*
> *Sitting, too, is Zen.*
> *If I speak or am silent,*
> *Tarry or hasten:*
> *Everything, in its true nature,*
> *Is stillness.*
>
> —SHODOKA

Passing on the Message

A famous Zen master was asked to define the true nature of Zen, but refused to say anything. Pressed for an answer, he said that he did not know what Zen was, and that, furthermore, no one could say what it was. When someone suggested that a teacher with so many students must surely know, if anyone did, he stuck to what he had said, but finally added: "Saying what Zen 'is' is as different from real Zen as saying what it feels like to put one's finger into boiling water is from actually doing it." What does this story mean? It means that

Zen can only be experienced personally and directly. And yet the message must still be passed on.

The way in which that message is presented—or can be presented—always depends on the level of consciousness of the actual or intended audience. There is no experience so private that it cannot stand up to everyday language, familiar images, and healthy common sense, and no mystery that cannot be conveyed to outsiders if their religious roots are still intact and if, ideally, the charismatic origins of the religion are still effective. Even a simple account of a post-mental experience of Being can strike an answering chord when it touches the pre-mental presence of Being in people who have reached the "mental" stage of human development, but have not entirely lost contact with Being. Today we have reached the mental stage in the West, but Being still touches us directly if we respond to it from the primal depths of our consciousness. If we rely on objective consciousness when we look at a religious doctrine, its logic may well convince us and its ethic attract us—but its real meaning will elude us. The more deeply our perception of reality is colored by the systems and restrictions of rational consciousness, the surer we are to miss the hidden meaning when it comes to us in a form that we can "understand."

This is why talking and writing "about" Zen is always a risky business. As Alan Watts rightly says: "In writing about Zen there are two extremes to be avoided: the one to define and explain so little that the reader is completely bewildered, and the other to define and explain so much that the reader thinks he understands Zen!"[7] And yet, as long as Zen exists, people will carry on trying to gain an insight into the nature of the Zen experience and to pass this insight on to others. The only question is—how?

We can understand the teachings of Zen only by keeping our eyes firmly fixed on the experience that is its starting point and its destination. By any standards, the Zen experi-

7. Alan Watts, *The Spirit of Zen* (New York: Grove Press, 1960).

ence is immensely worth having, and Zen teaching does us a genuine service by giving us an insight into this experience, into how we can have it and how it affects us. If, however, the insight is divorced from the experience, it sinks back into the realm of abstract theory and philosophical debate.

We are having *experiences* all the time, but unless they lead to insight, they do nothing for us. Zen turns humanity's deepest experience into insight, and presents that insight in its teaching. But even this is not enough; *exercise* is still needed to make insight a living reality. Only exercise—the hard, unremitting exercise in which a person sets out to draw practical conclusions from his insight into the Zen experience and its causes—holds the key to progress. And so Zen is three things: *experience whose importance is recognized; insight that illuminates;* and *constant exercise.* Only these three things together are Zen, and without them there is no Zen. For Zen is not a matter of theory, but of *practice*—practice based on a certain type of experience and leading back to that experience. Zen is not a theory of life, but a *living practice.*

Living Zen

Masters and Students

What does Zen set out to do for us? To wake us to our Buddha-nature, our true nature. And so we perform certain exercises to achieve a state of mind and being in which we can see ourselves in our true nature and manifest that true nature in and through ourselves to others. Our aim is to allow the Absolute within us to shine through; Zen's aim is to remove all the obstacles and help this to happen.

To practice Zen we need three kinds of knowledge: (1)

we must know that satori—the experience that subsumes a person in his true nature—is possible; (2) we must know what it is that separates us from our true nature; (3) we must know the way that leads from concealment of true nature to experience and manifestation of it.

Any practice that sets out to remake us depends for success on one thing: our knowing what it is that stands in the way of awakening and renewal. And what is that obstacle? The defining ego, whose consciousness and life-system shape our thoughts, feelings, and actions when we identify with it. Thus, Zen's central purpose is to stop us identifying with the ego, to shatter the ego and its carapace and to overthrow its value-system.

All Zen exercises share the same initial aim: to subvert the objective ego and its values and, by doing so, to pull from underneath our feet the ground that prevents us from making contact with the true ground of existence. This is where masters come in. Zen without masters is unthinkable. All Zen texts tell us how masters embody and transmit the meaning and purpose of Zen, and all Eastern wisdom is the wisdom of the masters, showing their students the way—the way that redeems them from the ego and frees them into their true nature. In the West today, there is a burning need to find this way, and as it grows sharper, so the call for masters grows louder.

Zen masters are unrelenting and harsh. If anything is fixed, it must be overthrown. If we lay claim to anything, that claim is rejected. If we cling to anything, it is torn from us. If we are proud of anything, it is held up to ridicule. Our illusions regarding ourselves are stripped bare. When we think we know something, it is made to seem absurd. And there are no lengths—no lengths whatsoever—to which a master will not go. He says and does things that we cannot begin to understand until we have grasped the lofty purpose that justifies it all: the senseless answer, the sudden onslaught, the well-aimed blow, the jarring shock, the punch in the face, the thump on the ear, the grating insult, the mocking laugh, the terrifying scream, the things that the ego cannot accept and yet must accept, the things that make the gorge rise and yet must be swallowed, the things that take us by surprise and knock us sideways, demolishing everything on which our normal picture of the world and ourselves has taught us to rely for support, uplift, and security. It is precisely when the ground is pulled away and we plummet that we may suddenly sense a truth outside our normal way of seeing, and realize that the fixed values that used to be the whole story and formerly defined our own position are simply the objective correlative of a subjective stance that our own finite understanding has determined, and that has therefore cut us off from something that can never be determined.

But to do all of this a master still needs one thing, without which he cannot function: a student. And when can a person call himself a student?

A person can call himself a student only when he is consumed with longing, when anguish has brought him to the ultimate barrier and he feels that he must break through it or die.

He can call himself a student only when restlessness of heart holds him fast and will not let him go until he finds a way of stilling it.

He can call himself a student only when he has set foot on the way, knows that he cannot turn back, and is willing to be led forward and obey.

He can call himself a student only when he is capable of unquestioning faith, can follow without understanding, and is ready to face and endure any trial.

He can call himself a student only when he can be hard with himself and is prepared to leave everything for the sake of the One, which is forcing its way within him toward the light.

It is only when the unconditional has seized him that he can accept every condition and endure all the hardships of the way on which the master leads him.

ALL OR NOTHING is written in large characters above

the door through which the student passes on his way to the exercise room. He must leave everything behind, but can take one certainty with him: it is not caprice that awaits him, but the clearsighted wisdom of the master, who focuses unwaveringly on what he really is and spares no effort to bring it to life; a kind of dying is expected of him, but its meaning is not death, but Life beyond life and death; not the destruction of existence, but Being that irradiates it. This is the meaning of the way that the master shows his student.

Heart to Heart

What to say, what to do, how to behave when one wishes to reveal Being to another person, who "naturally" thinks and lives in ways that conceal it from him? This is the question that has always confronted the prophets of Being, and to which the Zen masters have found their own answers. And it is precisely the finding of constant new solutions to this problem that is Zen's most typical feature. How does the Zen master set about leading his student toward the experience of Being? Formal instruction is not the most important part of the process. Overall, what really counts is communication from heart to heart, from true nature to true nature—from Being, which I *am* in my true nature, to Being, which every other person also *is* in his true nature.

A Zen teacher in the East cares nothing about his student's past. He ignores complexes and dreams. He is not a psychoanalyst, and he does not behave like a teacher. He does not probe, correct, or advise. He is filled with the One and focuses solely on the One. He looks only at what his student really is, feels his way toward it from what he really is himself, loves it, tries to make contact with it, and drives unwaveringly forward in search of it. For him, everything that blocks the student's true nature is summed up in one fatal error: a clinging to things that the student regards as unchanging and that stop him from changing himself. This is the root of the evil, and it must be torn out completely. Everything the master says and does thus bursts spontaneously and directly from the realm of the "undetermined" and sets out to liberate the undetermined in his students too. This is a matter of instant, here-and-now contact, for this is the only type of contact that reflects the everlasting *now* and in which the student can receive the lightning-stroke of revelation, smashing through the system that has thus far held him prisoner. Every familiar image, every well-worn concept, every merely conventional description of evil is dangerous. Only speech or silence, action or inaction, which comes here and now, once and unrepeatably, from the heart—from direct contact with the One—can get through to the student, touch on the presence of Being within him, wake it, and bring it to the light.

I remember what my own master said when I expressed the fear that his concepts and images might not help me much with Europeans: "You've got it wrong! Either you understand or you don't. If you don't, every concept, every image you use will be meaningless. If you do, you will always find your own way—find the word, gesture, or even silence that will touch the other person at that moment, break through his wall, reach his true nature, and, depending on his temperament and maturity, enable him to take the next step." This is what Zen is! Every word, every action has meaning and value only at a particular moment, in a specific situation. The fixed concepts and images of conventional religious practice and teaching often dam the living spring, so we should not be shocked when we hear that countless Zen students, after a lifetime of studying the scriptures and kneeling before the Buddha's image, have burned those scriptures and smashed that image once satori has brought them the direct experience of Being.

Stillness and Silence

The first means that a Zen master uses to prepare and open his student to the experience of Being is *silence.*

Silence as the path to experience in which a person senses the presence of Being in himself is practiced in the art of meditation, i.e., silent concentration in zazen. This exercise has its roots in an entire culture of stillness, which is typical of the East in general and Zen in particular.

Silent contemplation is the central element in the life of monks, but sitting in silence is not practiced only in monasteries. It is, on the contrary, a natural part of life in the East, whenever it respects the old traditions. But even in the East, only those who know what they are looking for find the greatest treasure it has to offer: contact with what we really are.

All the masters tell us that the reality of life—which our noisy waking consciousness prevents us from hearing—speaks to us chiefly in silence. "In the working of the Eastern mind," says Suzuki, "there is something calm, quiet, silent, undisturbable, which appears as if always looking into eternity. This quietude and silence, however, does not point to mere idleness or inactivity. . . . It is the silence of an 'eternal abyss' in which all contrasts and conditions are buried; it is the silence of God who, deeply absorbed in contemplation of his works past, present, and future, sits calmly on his throne of absolute oneness and allness. . . . Woe unto those who take it for decadence and death, for they will be overwhelmed by an overwhelming outburst of activity out of the eternal silence."[8] This stillness is also the stillness of Zen. It is the stillness of the unfathomable fountainhead and source of all belief, which can never be obscured because it is the point at which life, transcending all concepts and images, originates, and this is also why no concept, image, or question can penetrate it.[9]

There is hardly anything that Westerners have more

8. Suzuki, *Introduction to Zen Buddhism.*
9. Karlfried Graf Dürckheim, *The Japanese Cult of Tranquillity* (London: Rider, 1974).

trouble in finding or more difficulty in practicing than stillness. Noise assails us on all sides—outside noise but, even more, inner noise: our anxieties, our stifled feelings, our repressed urges, our impulses, our longings, and, above all, our turbulent distress at losing contact with our imprisoned true nature. We are used to noise, expect it, and often cannot live without it—even using it to soothe our everyday worries. For comfort we look to multiplicity, which thunders in and around us, and miss the One, which we vitally need but which reveals itself only in stillness. The thought of coming face to face with ourselves terrifies us. And this is precisely what sitting in silence is intended to do: to make us face up to ourselves and our true nature and—on our way to that encounter—to everything that separates us from it.

There is also the stillness that speaks and is born of silence, but speaks only if we bear the silence patiently and focus our whole attention on the answer. In moments of black despair, we have all prayed to God for an answer—and God, instead of answering, has remained silent and, remaining silent, has thrust us deeper into the darkness. And then, if we hold out without complaining, the answer suddenly comes from this silence and floods us with light. And yet what is more alien to our normal way of hearing than absolute silence? Divine truth, however, does not speak to us in our normal language. And it is precisely the silence that confronts us when all our expectations are focused on a spoken answer that can suddenly rouse us to consciousness. This is something that Zen masters know.

There are countless Zen stories in which a student, filled with a passionate longing, comes to his master for an answer to the one question that sums up and expresses all his seeking, all his anguish. The master receives him. The great, all-deciding moment has come. The master knows himself that everything is at stake. What will he say? The student puts his question, waits breathlessly for the answer, and the unexpected happens: the master looks at him—steadily, piercingly—and says nothing! His silence has the weight, the solidity of bronze.

And realization hits the student like a thunderbolt. The entire edifice on which his question was based collapses. And something that questions cannot reach rushes into him. Burning, reeling, weeping, laughing, he wakes to the truth. One well-known example is the story of Master Juchi, which Hermann Hesse put into verse for Wilhelm Gundert when the latter's great book, *Bi-Yan-Lu*, [10] was published:

> Master Juchi had, so people say,
> A peaceful, kindly, unassuming way,
> Was never heard to speak and never taught,
> For words are but illusions, and he sought
> To keep illusions faithfully at bay.
> And so, while others chose to air their learning,
> While novices and monks spoke out concerning
> The meaning of the world, its why and wherefore,
> And boldly found for each "because" a "therefore,"
> He listened and said nothing, always turning
> A warning finger upward, and the same
> Was his response whenever people came—
> Questioners who, careless or perplexed,
> Inquired as to the meaning of some text,
> The dawning of the truth or Buddha's name.
> Silent but eloquent, this pointing finger
> Grew ever more insistent, more commanding;
> Instructing, guiding, praising, reprimanding,
> Of the world's meaning and of truth it spoke
> So well that many a pupil, understanding
> Its gentle message, suddenly awoke.

Silence can wake us only when it shatters everything that prevents us from experiencing Being. The chain that binds us snaps only when it is stretched to the breaking point—and beyond. That is why silence can produce this effect

10. *Bi-Yan-Lu, Meister Yüan-wu's Niederschrift von der smaragdenen Felswand,* translated into German with a commentary by Wilhelm Gundert (Munich: C. Hanser Verlag, 1960). Using original texts, this book provides the genuine seeker with a unique introduction to the mystery of Zen. It is the fundamental work on Zen.

only when it destroys the ground on which the questioner stands, and when the question itself is the distillation of a lifetime's quest and the seeker's whole life depends on it. The stories of the masters' silence and its impact on students cannot be understood unless this is the situation—unless the anguish of a lifetime is concentrated in the question and everything hinges on the answer. And what is true of silence is also true of the other means a master uses to help his students.

The Discipline of Silence

One way of leading a student on the path of Zen is to destroy all the concepts and images he uses to "grasp" the truth. This prevents him from confusing the image with the thing—"the finger pointing at the moon with the moon itself"—and it also prevents him from resting complacently on fixed ideas. If, during an instruction period, the student repeats something the master has just said, the master makes fun of him and says the opposite. When a saying is repeated, it ceases to be true; this applies even to the wise sayings of antiquity. This is why masters are often so harsh, even savage, in their comments on other masters' utterances. Nothing that is said about the truth can or must be said once and for all—even something said by a master, which becomes lifeless and positively harmful when it is parroted by someone else. A verbal bomb thrown at our assumptions must not be recycled as a pillow for more of those assumptions. When a master sees that his student is close to the truth, or has even tasted it already, his severity only increases. An example: A student returns from a pilgrimage on which satori has come to him. He respectfully approaches his master, who receives him in silence, and kneels down before him. Just as he is raising his head and preparing to speak, the master lifts his stick and deals him thirty heavy blows in quick succession. "Why have you done this, master?" asks the student. "I said nothing." "Even a word," replies the master, "and it would have been too late!" By stopping him from putting his experience into words, the master saves him from losing the treasure contained in that experience.

Another example: The student enters the master's room, and the master sees at once that he has experienced satori. He puts him to one last test. The student kneels without speaking and the master says to him amiably, "And so, now you have it!" "Yes, master, I have it," the hapless student replies. "You have nothing!" roars the master. "Get out of my sight!"

The old wisdom of the mystics—to see as if we did not see, to have as if we did not have, to do as if we did not do! But how hard this is, and how much harder for us than for the Oriental, who is less obsessed with the need to define and make everything definite. We have all had the heartrending experience of seeing feelings simply melt away because someone has tried to "understand" them and put them into words—or because we have done so ourselves. Perhaps we are lost in contemplation of a landscape, a sunrise, a flower, totally at one with what we are seeing and feeling and deeply aware of the fullness of Being in a way that only happens when all the barriers are down. Suddenly someone pops up beside us and says, "How beautiful!" And life seems to split down the middle. We are back within ourselves, and "beauty" is somewhere else—outside! Whatever it was that linked us with beauty in its true nature and ours has gone, and cannot be called back.

If this is true of everyday feelings, it is still truer of those fragile experiences in which Being touches us because we are suddenly open to its constant presence. I remember a dream I once had. I had gone into a church. People were milling around on all sides, and a tourist guide was showing them a small bronze figure of Christ. Suddenly one of its outstretched arms turned in my direction. I seized its hand, and was instantly filled with a feeling I cannot begin to describe. Being, in all its fullness, seemed to be flooding through me. Everything seemed totally meaningful and clear, and I was conscious of being completely sheltered, utterly at peace.

Then I suddenly started to wonder. I withdrew slightly and the question "What is this?" began to shape itself faintly in my mind. At once, the little statue crumbled into dust—simply disappeared! I had lost everything. Fear surged up in me and I woke to a sense of utter desolation and guilt. This is the way things are; there is a reality that disappears as soon as we define it, as soon as we ask what it is. Indeed, barely voicing the question is enough to dispel something that was there just a moment before.

This realization underlies all of Zen's vital utterances and greatly increases its significance for us; for if we are looking for something that can be "defined" beyond all doubt, we desperately need someone to tell us that this kind of seeking is actually concealing the truth of Life from us.

Paradox

Naturally we tend to see the world in terms of the objective knowledge that questions such as "What is this?" set out to provide. How hard it is to let Being in without at once losing it again by allowing objective consciousness to focus on it— but this is precisely where the inner way can help us.

If the foundations we stand on in natural consciousness actually prevent us from experiencing Being, then the master who wants to lead us to that experience must first do everything he can to knock them away. This is why his actions often startle like bolts from the blue, why he speaks in riddles, why shock tactics are his tenderness and nonsense his logic.

The student asks, "What does the 'coming of Bodhidharma' mean?" The master answers, "The oak tree in the courtyard." Another student asks, "What is Buddha?" The master replies, "There never was one!" Some more examples:

> The pupil asks, "What is everyday living?"
> The master raises his fly whisk.
> "Is that it?" inquires the monk.

84

"What is that?" says the master.
The monk makes no answer.
"What is the present moment?"
"No one ever asked me that before."
"I am asking now, master."
"You fool!"

There are countless answers like this—answers apparently senseless and exasperating. What are they supposed to mean? Is it easy or hard to work that meaning out? As long as we keep asking "What is this?" we remain the prisoners of our worldly consciousness, which, precisely because it is worldly, holds the supra-worldly at bay. The same applies to "When?" or "Where?" Life lies beyond the "five *W*'s"—*who, what, when, where, why;* it "cannot be questioned," says Meister Eckhart. The answers to all these questions define something, project it onto objective, static consciousness, and reduce life to facts. Without facts, people feel lost. But what is to become of them if their reliance on facts is really total, and they see their own lives only in terms that turn every living thing into a "fact"? Being and their true nature are barred to them. If reality is to get through to us, we must learn to turn our backs on everything that cuts us off from it. When it claims to be absolute, objective consciousness becomes a wall, and we can tear it down only by daring to trust the truth of the intangible, numinous something that breathes in our deepest experience, avoiding any attempt to pin that experience down. This is why the hole punched in the tidy fabric of "objective" reality by the master's paradoxical answer can also become the aperture through which the great light sheds a first unexpected ray on the seeker.

Practicing Zen

The Meaning of Exercise

The East speaks to us in its wise books, but it speaks to us even more clearly today in the exercises it teaches us to follow, telling us that working on ourselves in this way will turn us into something more. But what does "more" mean? Different people offer different answers.

In fact, most people who follow these exercises today use them to restore or improve their performance or health, to become more efficient and give themselves a better grip on life. This is certainly useful, but has nothing to do with what Zen means by practice.

Hatha yoga, for instance, is taken up in this practical spirit and taught as a kind of calisthenics. This is undoubtedly good for people's health, improves their concentration, and makes them feel better in an everyday sense, but it no longer has anything to do with yoga's real meaning. Yoga is not meant to make a person more efficient or to help him develop "higher faculties," but to "yoke" him to divine reality.

People who want worldly power are often attracted, however, by the miracles of so-called yogis who have actually stopped being yogis and become fakirs instead. Even in the East, the aberration of wanting to work wonders is not uncommon. I once asked a Zen teacher what he thought of the wonders worked by Indian "yogis," and he said: "When a person spends years or decades developing certain physical or spiritual powers, he can always do things that strike others as wonderful at the end of it. But what has that got to do with the inner way? It's the other way round: If a person is practic-

86

ing on the *way* and toward the *way,* he finds himself able to do seemingly miraculous things as time goes on, first in his own field of exercise, and later beyond it. But this is not what the exercise is about. The exercise is about his progress on the inner way, and that is what it points to."

Thus, a fundamental distinction is needed between exercises that serve the world-ego, i.e., pragmatic exercises, and exercises that serve the self-realization of our true nature. We can call these initiation exercises, which open the door to Mystery—the Mystery being in fact "true nature," the unfathomable center of all things. Coming to inner awareness of this center, dissolving in it, and making it the basis of everything we do is what all Zen exercises aim at.

Some exercises, however, seem to be helping us toward the center when they are actually leading us even more dangerously astray—breathing, relaxation, posture, and meditation exercises that temporarily dissipate tension and frustration, soothing us and making us feel, wrongly, as if we have made some progress on the inner way.[11] As long as the world-ego retains its grip, all that such exercises do is treacherously to encourage a state of mind and being that reinforces that ego.

Even Zen exercises can easily be misread as aiming at worldly efficiency or even miraculous feats. Stories like those of the master swordsman who freezes his opponent's suspended weapon in the air with a look, the master archer who scores a perfect bull's-eye in the dark and splits his first arrow with a second,[12] the master who wakes a dead man to life and brings a bird tumbling dead to the ground with one shout: true though they are, they can easily mislead us, if we are ruled by the ambitious world-ego, into taking up Zen exercises in the hope of achieving similar feats ourselves. But if we approach them like this, we are misunderstanding them and missing what they have to offer us.

11. Cf. Karlfried Graf Dürckheim, *Hara: The Vital Centre of Man,* trans. Sylvia-Monica von Kospoth and Estelle Healey (London: Unwin Paperbacks, 1977).
12. Eugen Herrigel, *Zen in the Art of Archery* (New York: Random House, 1971).

And it is equally easy, if it is only the world you care about, to misunderstand the Zen practice of seated meditation—zazen—and assume that its purpose is to help you to continue to lead your old life, but in a more relaxed, detached, and "serene" way.

This way the meaning and spirit of Zen practice are missed, and so is the answer it can bring to the vital aspiration of people in the West—the longing to feel true nature break through, to manifest it freely in everything they do and so become full human beings for the first time.

Zen exercise never tries merely to increase a person's knowledge or skills while leaving him otherwise unchanged, but sets out to make him over, waking him to his true nature and transforming him from it. And so all Zen exercises center upon the turning point of human transformation, upon satori, the Great Experience, in which the old ego disappears, true nature emerges, and the individual, transformed to himself, returns into the world in which he now bears witness to Being—knowing, creating, and loving in a new way.

To practice Zen is to work in a disciplined way toward a state of mind and being in which the Absolute is fully present and takes on form within us, while its all-embracing unity is experienced directly and becomes creatively active. How is this state of mind and being reached? By integrating the here-and-now ego with true nature and Being beyond the here-and-now. Its purpose? To bear witness to Being in here-and-now existence. The state of oneness we achieve when we are "integrated with Being" in Zen is not, therefore, just a matter of renouncing the world and disappearing in the Absolute. It is also a matter of returning to the world—now permanently at one with true nature and truly ourselves through contact with Being—and preserving that contact by acting in a manner consonant with Being. What, then, does "Zen work" consist of?

Dismantling the Ego

"Zen work" aims at achieving ever deeper contact and union with our true nature and—once the breakthrough comes and the new consciousness awakens (satori)—at taking form from and bearing witness to this true nature in our daily life and work. The turning point is satori. The precondition is the *dismantling of the ego.*

Dismantling the ego! People hearing this today react in very different ways, and with very mixed feelings. Many reject the whole notion out of hand. Psychologists are quick to suggest that too little—not too much—ego is far more of a problem than we think. And many people see in the fundamental call to "drop the ego" the typically Oriental danger of losing individuality, abandoning a cornerstone of European thought, vanishing into nothingness, and dissolving in the All-One. Anthroposophists are afraid of losing their "Christ impulse from the ego." None of this is the case. Zen is not in the business of destroying the ego, but of transforming the merely world-centered ego and changing the person determined solely by that ego into a person determined by his true nature. Nor does Zen reject the world, but merely attachment to the world.

When it speaks of "dismantling the ego," Zen is speaking—in full agreement with the Western spiritual tradition —of the basic condition we must fulfill to become truly ourselves and shape our lives in a manner consonant with Being. Dismantling the ego in this sense means chiefly dismantling the puny, power-hungry, self-assertive, and possessive ego, which is always anxiously focused on its own survival, status, and success. Even in the "objective" sphere, we all know that we cannot do anything worth doing or even emerge as "personalities"—integrated members of the community, sharing its values, attitudes, and aspirations—as long as this ego exists.

But dismantling the ego in Zen is not simply something we must do to live and think as members of the community. It is something we must do to release our spirituality—and this may be even harder if we are anchored in objective, logical, aesthetic, and ethical values than if we are anchored in the self-seeking ego. The more selfish a person is, the likelier he is to run headlong to disaster and, having touched bottom, to hear and heed the call to another way of life. The more rational and ethical he is, the greater the danger that his justified existence (justified because it accords with accepted norms and values) will retain its stultifying hold and so cut him off from real life—for even virtue, once it becomes a rigid system, is inimical to life.

Zen, like all Buddhism, sees attachment as the real root of evil, and people as evil to the extent that attachment makes them so. Attachment prevents us from thinking or living in better ways, and so cuts us off from the creative, redeeming power of life. This means that enlightenment, too, is possible only when attachment has been overcome. The three basic human failings that Buddhism repeatedly emphasizes—ignorance, desire, and hatred—are themselves mere offshoots of attachment.

Attachment always aims at possession. It is rooted in the hunger for permanence, the search for something fixed; it makes people hang on to anything they have once possessed, known, or been able to do. To "love" in this sense means to cling so tightly that one cannot let go. Once our notions and images of life set firm, we are "fixed" by them and cannot escape them. Images, of course, have gained in respect what barren logic has lost—rightly so, since it is in images and from them that life ripens into form. But images, once they harden and set, make it even harder for life to develop and mature; indeed, images and notions are often more effective than concepts in keeping the breath of life out. There is, however, a third and possibly even greater danger: ways of thinking, moving, and speaking that have become habitual and cannot be changed. It is as if people feared that their egos (and they themselves) would be catastrophically threatened by the giving up of ingrained gestures or harmful mannerisms—for instance, the permanently hunched shoulders in which a distrustful, fearful, or overweening ego takes refuge.

The fixed element is the worldview and life-style locked into concepts, images, and attitudes that have congealed and solidified. The fixing element is the defining ego, the "builder and guardian of the dwelling." This is why Zen practice always starts by dismantling the objective, defining ego, the ego concerned with possession and self-assertion, the ego that avoids pain, seeks pleasure, and distrusts everything, the ego that is constantly repeating the things it has once learned to do.

In the defining, attached ego, the indwelling fullness of what we *are* in our true nature is transformed into the objective multiplicity of what we *have.* Zen gives us back to our true nature.

Zen teaches us that there are two ways of neutralizing the ego: wearing out its energy by pushing objective thought or action to extremes, or totally withdrawing it from objective activity through meditation. Everything turns on experiencing and enduring nothingness, the void—for only in the void can the fullness, form, energy, and unity of Being be revealed.

The basic Zen exercise is zazen.[13] In Rinzai Zen there is also, chiefly, the koan, a problem the student is given to think out, but cannot solve by thinking. It is only when a person is at his wits' end that he is sufficiently shaken to see that he is on the wrong track. It is only when he reaches the breaking point that the inner eye opens and the consciousness that reveals him to himself as Being is released.

When this new consciousness is born, he continues to see the world objectively, but the objective vision is suddenly charged with deeper meaning, and he senses that his whole life is anchored in Being which *is*—beyond life and death, self and world, any and every "this and that." This process of transformation is also served by exercises in which a particular

13. Hugo Makibi Enomiya-Lassalle, *Zen: Way to Enlightenment* (New York: Taplinger Publishing Co., 1968).

skill is practiced to a point of completion that is not the product of ability, but the fruit of maturity that the adept attains by disciplining, dying to, and coming to himself again.

This is where the old Japanese exercises come in—archery, fencing, spear fighting, all the martial arts. So, too, do the tea ceremony and flower arranging. In all of these, correct breathing, correct balance, and correct stillness help to remake the individual. The basic aim is always the same: by tirelessly practicing a given skill, the student finally sheds the ego with its fears, worldly ambitions, and reliance on objective scrutiny—sheds it so completely that he becomes the instrument of a deeper power, from which mastery falls instinctively, without further effort on his part, like a ripe fruit. Whenever a person succeeds in ridding himself of the ego and becoming a pure instrument, he frees Being, which is striving all the time to manifest itself in him, allowing it to sing its everlasting song through his particular skill. And the more he identifies with what he experiences and expresses in that skill, the more fruitful and real it becomes throughout his everyday life.

The Purpose of Technique

The point of every exercise in which a specific skill is practiced is not improved performance as such, but what happens to the performer. Improved performance remains, of course, the immediate goal—but the point is the person achieving it, who purifies and transforms himself by seeking to perfect the exercise in the right way. What practice means in this case is not at all what it means when performance per se is the issue. Practiced in the right spirit, as a means to the *way*, exercise changes a person completely; his transformation then becomes not just necessary, but sufficient to perfect his performance. Skill always shows that a person has practiced, but the special kind of skill that goes with Zen's sublime teaching shows that Being has made over a person and itself expresses the change. This is why the East speaks of a Tao of technique, in which Tao and technique become one within the individual, so that technique expresses Tao.

The most striking account of the change wrought in a person by prolonged practice of a skill is given by Eugen Herrigel in his book on Zen archery. He shows that archery, "to the extent that it is a contest of the archer with himself," is a life-and-death matter. Why? Because it is an exercise in which "fundamentally the marksman aims at himself and may even succeed in hitting himself."

Endless repetition is common to all the exercises. Total concentration is needed at first, but as the actions slowly become automatic, the ego/object tension, which is rooted in purposive effort, gradually relaxes until ego and object (the implement, the instrument, but also the skill itself as process) become one, and the objective, defining, purposive consciousness is separated out and totally neutralized. Only when purposive tension is no longer necessary can its vehicle—the ego—be neutralized. And only when the ego disappears can the spirit (in the sense of supra-personal energy) come into play and mastery burst unchecked and as if of its own accord from the adept's true nature. At this point, mastery is no longer the product of conscious effort, but the revelation of true nature in a particular exercise.

The stages in the process, as described by Herrigel, are as follows: relaxing completely and shedding all tension, concentrating utterly, penetrating the mystery of breathing, mastering the "form" (external technique) completely through endless repetition, allowing the "spirit" to open so that the arrow can be loosed without effort, "devaluing" all interest (not merely in hitting the target, but also in inner progress)— all of this shielded, sustained, and carried forward solely by constant, tireless exercise, endlessly repeated and ever more unquestioning. Persistent exercise is the barrier that brings many people to grief. Not all the exercises are hard in themselves, but doing them properly is hard.

Practice, as Zen means it and Herrigel describes it, opens up a way that we in the West would be well advised to follow. No longer merely the means to a skill, it becomes a means of helping ourselves and others to break through to our true nature and give it form in the world. Seen in this way, exercise becomes a vehicle for the one really helpful form of guidance, and any exercise centered on personal transformation—on a person's being reborn to himself and his own creative potential, on manifesting his true nature in everything he does—comes close to Zen.

The turning point in exercise comes when our attention shifts from objective notions and goals to the mood, attitude, and movement that come from within and can only be inwardly sensed. This gives a new meaning to certain therapeutic practices that have been used so far mainly to restore health and productive energy. Drawing and painting, often used as therapy, provide one example. Practiced in the Zen spirit, they do not merely serve a diagnostic or generally liberating function, but become part of a calculated process leading a person to himself. Maria Hippius has described that process like this: "Anyone who practices drawing as a means of self-improvement can become aware of certain basic creative energies within himself and develop toward something that comes to him as a fundamental inner experience. In this way, he can gain a new 'understanding' of himself and of the world through essential and substantial experiences that he procures and brings to consciousness through the senses rather than the mind. Practiced in the right way, drawing can help him to see that his errors are errors along the way to becoming a full human being, and that he cannot become fully himself until he has made contact with his true nature and found his way back to the force that really sustains him.

"Like any therapeutic exercise, therapeutic drawing sets out to wake a person who has ground to an unproductive halt, gradually bring into play a new vital impetus, and call forth basic impulses, thereby mobilizing something deeper and stronger in his consciousness and conduct than the 'realities' by which he has previously attempted to live. His scarred and twisted persona, his failures and his apprehensions—all the things that cut him off from reality and truth—are allowed to fall away as the primal forces of Being gradually submerge them. Powers deep within his own nature may be mobilized, progressively shaping his own inner core and revealing his innermost potential as an individual. Stultifying complexes and inertia are replaced by a mysterious 'impetus from Being,' an impetus that is certainly weak to start with, but gradually gathers momentum—an impulse that comes from true nature and is caused (but now in the fullest sense) by the very same person who seemed to have reached a dead end.

"To achieve this result, the exercise of drawing, writing (graphotherapy), painting, or modeling must have a meditative, ritual character. No healing activity can succeed unless transcendence, i.e., the patient's true nature, is kept firmly in view. In the same way, no activity can successfully harness a person's inner powers and bring his full potential to light unless it has a 'sacred' character. It can precipitate the decisive change only if it comes from deep down, where the person is his undivided self, and only if every brushstroke is completely meant. This is the only way in which rediscovered sense qualities can revitalize him and restore the very special interplay of forces on which he depends. The adept suddenly senses, tastes, hears, and sees what is coming into being in and from himself, and discovers an entirely new inner mode of moving and perceiving in his minute, seemingly trivial activity, which he now learns to exploit for what it contains of Being and of quality."[14]

What is true of creative activity is also true of every physical exercise, for example, the practice of correct breathing, posture, and movement. It is only when mistakes in posture and breathing caused by defects in a person's life-style and by interference from the ego have been overcome, and the objective-purposive consciousness has receded, that true nature becomes an indwelling presence and is free to open and

14. Maria Hippius, "Das geführte Zeichen," in M. Hippius, ed., *Transzendenz als Erfahrung* (Munich: O. W. Barth-Verlag, 1966).

develop. We must learn to see all our movements from within as significant gestures. We must find out if and how far we ourselves are really present in our actions, or are merely the prisoners of convention and guided by certain fixed ideas in everything we say and do. We must be able to sense what it means to be fully present, from our true nature, in every movement, brushstroke, and gesture. This means that any activity—not just activities requiring special skills, but repetitive activities in office, kitchen, workshop, or factory—can be turned into an exercise. "Daily exercise" acquires a very special meaning when everything becomes a field for exercise in Zen, from the right way of breathing, walking (to be what we really are, we must walk "from" the right center), standing, sitting, speaking, and writing, to any working activity that uses technique. The only things that count are the basic approach and attitude.

Westerners usually regard the opening up of true nature and the self-fulfillment that results as a wholly "inner" process, and may well be surprised that the body is expected to play such an important part. Of course, the body in question is not the body we *have*, but the body we *are*. From the standpoint of the true self, there is both a right and a wrong way of being present in this body, the physical medium through which we express and manifest ourselves—in which we are "embodied." Our way of being present, of "being there," expresses what we are in a total sense, transcending the body/soul antithesis.[15] Working on a person's way of "being there" always means working on what he is in a total sense, in both soul and body. For this reason, too, all therapies that aim at self-realization but focus solely on the "psychological" element (i.e., psychoanalysis) will soon be completely outmoded.

Anything that contains the primal substance undiminished can provide a useful starting point and field for exercise when we set out to rediscover and release our true nature.

15. Dürckheim, *Hara: The Vital Centre of Man.*

This is particularly true of primal sense experience: color, sound, smell, touch, taste, and—above all—bodily awareness. But it is not just a matter of rediscovering primal, pre-personal experience. On the contrary, the original sense-qualities, when they are experienced in meditation, develop a new supra-sensual depth. Experienced and understood in this way, they form one of the roots of the supra-sensual spirit that unlocks the fullness of life. Instead of being taken for granted as an automatic part of all experience and disregarded, they must be raised to consciousness, seen for what they are, and recognized as playing a vital part in the discovery and development of the real self. This is perhaps even truer of bodily awareness and movement sensed from within. Every entrenched neurosis expresses itself in the body and strikes even deeper roots in its physical symptoms. A neurotic is a person who cannot find himself in his own body. And this is why coming to terms with one's own body—first becoming aware of bad habits and then freeing oneself from them—is an important factor in healing, indeed a vital one.

A person "is there" in the right way, is personally present in the true sense, when he mediates effectively between the Absolute and the relative, between Being and existence. Existence rooted in Being is what counts, and this is what Zen teaches. But the fundamental exercise is zazen.

Zazen

Any account of Zen, however brief, must give zazen—the central Zen exercise—its due.

Notwithstanding the many Zen, particularly Rinzai Zen, exercises that bring action into meditation, sitting is still the basic exercise: sitting in the right position, sitting quietly, sitting and meditating—zazen.

The student of Zen begins and ends the day with zazen. And during the day, whenever he has time—and the further he goes, the more time he finds—he practices zazen. Even at night, if he wakes without falling asleep again at once, he sits up and does zazen. Zazen is not meditating on a sacred saying or image, but just sitting and trying to shed all images and thoughts, actively trying to enter the void.

Westerners may at first be surprised that something that looks so much like doing nothing should play such an important—indeed a vital—part in bringing our real humanity to fruition in *the true self.* But it does, and is important not only to those who believe that the purpose and goal of all spiritual exercise is union with the Absolute—but equally to those who believe that this union vitalizes our way of living, loving, and creating *in the world,* and gives it deeper meaning. For the world is always our ultimate touchstone in the West, and even people who have attained final maturity, and have been transformed and liberated into Being beyond space and time, must bear witness to Being in the here-and-now.

We can no more say what zazen *is* than we can say what a sound, color, smell, taste, or hardness or softness is; we must hear, see, smell, taste, and touch it for ourselves. And so we must sit zazen for ourselves, and not just once but again and again—for weeks, months, and years—to know what it is or, more accurately, what it can be or, more accurately still, what we ourselves can gradually become with zazen's help and *be* even when we are not doing zazen. For zazen means and gives us something that is not there only while we are exercising, but always: an attitude that incorporates, expresses, and *is* Being, and which renews us and helps us to see new things in a new way and use every moment to the full, with Being constantly reflected in what we are (i.e., our way of "being there"), how we experience what we experience, and in the positive value of our actions—or, indeed, our omissions.

Practicing Zazen

One does zazen for the reason one does any genuinely spiritual exercise: to achieve union with something the Christian would call God, the Hindu Brahma, and the Buddhist . . .

Of the three, the Buddhist takes the most care not to say what cannot be said. When he speaks of Buddha-nature, he is merely referring indirectly to the intangible heart of all things—Being, which is everything that is. Being drops out of consciousness as soon as we become conscious of something, but the sacred tranquility that lies beyond all feelings can make it a permanent, indwelling presence, bringing us home to the truth of what we are. To become aware of our true nature in this way is at once our own good fortune, our way of helping others, our business in life, and the purpose of exercising, i.e., of doing zazen.

The path to this awareness leads through emptiness, through total detachment from everything that fills the contingent consciousness that is governed by the concepts, systems, and images of contingent reality and prevents us from making the breakthrough. In zazen we are meant to shed all worldly objects and emotions, all images, notions, and concepts. But our normal "waking" state is governed by the ego, and the ego is *never* free of objects—and so our next problem is to free ourselves through exercise from the ego, which is synonymous with the presence of images, ideas, and thoughts, as well as desires, anxieties, feelings, hopes, and fears. The natural consciousness is always "preoccupied" (i.e., full to start with), and this is the greatest obstacle to direct contact with true nature, with Being. To be liberated from objective consciousness is not, however, to be "unconscious." On the contrary, it is to be present and awake in a new subjective consciousness, which is no longer concerned with what we have (in an objective sense), but with what we really *are*—our true nature as the mode in which Being, the true nature of all things, is individually present in every one of us. When true nature comes fully to consciousness, we can also see it in all the "objects" around us. This is our personal opportunity, our very own way of being in a present beyond space and time—the everlasting now—in the midst of contingent reality.

The Technique of Sitting

Technique may seem a strange word to use in connection with a spiritual exercise designed to put us in touch with Being, which lies beyond the reach of objective consciousness and purposive activity, both of which are essential to the learning and mastering of any technique. The contradiction in fact disappears once we realize that technique is used to create the conditions for the Absolute to manifest itself and that the activity, when it is mastered and becomes automatic, is performed perfectly without reference to the will (guided by objective consciousness). At this point, Life can flow unchecked from the adept's true nature; that is, it can live itself out and become apparent in the activity itself.

In its fullness, order, and unity, Life is the animating, regulating, and unifying force behind everything—and when Being takes on form in a person, it can manifest itself freely in that form. Endlessly redeeming and creating, Life can melt fixed forms down and reabsorb them, and at the same time bring formlessness to form in an everlasting process of becoming. It is precisely this creative and saving Life that we obstruct by taking on fixed contours and clinging to them. These are the obstacles that zazen sets out to remove.

The student of zazen can no more *make* the exercise succeed than a gardener can *make* his plants grow. But a gardener can and must create the conditions for growth, by removing everything that stops his plants from growing, and encouraging everything that helps them to develop. In the same way, the student of zazen must get rid of anything that prevents him from becoming a medium for Being, and foster anything that helps him.

The following three factors prevent indwelling transcendence from showing through:

1. "Static" consciousness, that is, consciousness that deals in, clings to, and is filled with fixed entities (definite images, thoughts, notions, concepts, attitudes, positions).

2. An attitude—a way of "being there," spiritually *and*

physically, that obstructs the all-transforming movement of Life. The impulses, urges, desires, and anxieties embodied in this kind of wrong attitude are either rigid and thus prevent a person from becoming a clear medium, or formless and free-floating and thus prevent Life from revealing itself as living form.

3. Wrong breathing. Correct breathing, the everlasting movement of change, is the fullest expression of life itself. Wrong breathing constricts this natural movement, but as it grows "righter," its rightness fills the consciousness, automatically bringing the individual into inner harmony with life's ever-changing rhythm.

Correct Posture

What Master Dogen, the founder of Soto Zen, had to say on correct zazen posture is still valid today:

"You prepare for exercise by laying a thick mat in the selected spot and placing a cushion on it to sit on. You may sit in either the *kekka-fuza* (full lotus) or *hanka-fuza* (half-lotus) position. In the first, you place your right foot on your left thigh and let it rest there, and you then place your left foot on your right thigh and let it rest there. In the second, you merely place your left foot on your right thigh. You should wear your clothing and belt loosely, but neatly. You next rest your right hand on your left leg, and your left hand on the palm of the right. You place your two thumbs together, tip to tip. You keep your body upright and carefully maintain a correct sitting posture by leaning neither to left nor right, neither forward nor back. You must also be careful to keep your ears directly above your shoulders, and your nose directly over your navel. Your tongue is held in contact with the roof of your mouth. Both your lips and teeth are closed. Your eyes should always be kept open. You breathe lightly in and out through your nose. In this way, you bring your body into the best position. You now take a deep breath and sway to left and right until you come to rest, firm as a rock, in an upright position. And now think about the unthinkable. How do you do that? By not thinking! And this is the deep and natural art of zazen."

The Zen master Hakuun Yasutani,[16] who died a short time ago, provided the following commentary:

" 'You sway to left and right until you come to rest, firm as a rock, in an upright position.' You move your body like a pendulum, first oscillating broadly and then gradually reducing the swing until the body eventually comes to rest in a central position of its own accord. You then sit firmly and enter the state of being motionless as a mountain. It is only at this point that your mind is collected (concentrated).

" 'Think about the unthinkable. How do you do that? By not thinking!' Beginners (and the meaning of the term 'beginner' depends on the yardstick applied) always have trouble with distracting thoughts during zazen. More advanced students, who are used to sitting, whose legs no longer hurt and who feel increasingly at ease, can become drowsy—and even those who normally get plenty of sleep readily fall into a kind of absent or abstracted state. These are the two diseases of consciousness. We call the first (persistent distracting thoughts) 'agitation,' or *sanran,* and the second (drowsiness or abstraction) 'somnolence,' or *kontin.* In zazen, consciousness is not supposed to vanish, but to enter a state of disciplined composure in which neither of these conditions can occur. Normally, consciousness moves so independently along its accustomed track that it is hard to keep an eye on it. That is why we must learn to avoid both agitation and somnolence. Both disappear if we approach the exercise in a really serious manner. Think of yourself as fighting a duel to the death, in which either you or your opponent will be killed. You stand facing each other with drawn swords. You cross blades. What is the point of complaining now that you are not completely on the spot, that insomnia has left you sleepy and confused?

16. Hakuun Yasutani was also the teacher of Philip Kapleau, author of *The Three Pillars of Zen* (New York: Anchor/Doubleday, 1980).

Even if you have never practiced zazen, this is one situation where no distracting thoughts will bother you—if your attention wanders for a moment, you will be cut down instantly. In the same way, anyone who seriously wants to attain the right state of consciousness for zazen can do it. If he fails, it is only because he is not really serious. It is distressing that we ordinary mortals should find it so hard to summon up the seriousness we need for zazen. To do it, we must bring our minds into the right state—and this is known as 'not-thinking' (the state that lies beyond the to-and-fro of conflicting opinions). It is, in fact, the central element in performing the exercise.''

A fuller description by Master Yasutani:

"First you must choose a quiet room to sit in. Take a mat which is about thirty-five inches square and not too soft, and place on it a small, round cushion, measuring approximately twelve inches across. Sit on the cushion and let your legs rest on the mat. You should not wear trousers, which make it hard for you to cross your legs. For many reasons, it is best to adopt the standard Buddhist posture (the full lotus). You do this by laying your right foot over your left thigh, and then your left foot over your right thigh. The main purpose of sitting like this is to achieve absolute stability, and you do this by establishing a broad, solid base and crossing your legs on this base, with both knees touching the mat. When the body is completely still, there is no movement to stimulate thought, and the mind also becomes still, as if of its own accord. If you find this position too difficult, you should adopt the half-lotus, simply laying your left foot over your right thigh. Westerners who are wholly unfamiliar with zazen may find even this too difficult; the knees will not stay down, and repeatedly have to be pressed down so that both touch the mat. If you find both the full and the half-lotus impossible, you should cross your legs in the normal way or simply use a chair.

"The next step is to place your right hand, palm upward, in your lap and to place your left hand, palm upward, in your right. Form a circle with your thumbs by bringing them together at the tip. You should remember that the right side of the body is the active side, and the left the passive. By laying the left foot on the right, you are suppressing the active side, and this makes for maximum tranquility. If you look at an image of Buddha, however, you will see that his posture is exactly the reverse—the right foot is on top. This is to show that a Buddha, unlike ourselves, is always active and saving others.

"When you have crossed your legs, lean forward, push your buttocks back, and slowly come back to an upright position. Your head should be straight, so that your ears are directly above your shoulders, and the tip of your nose directly over your navel. From the waist up, your body should be weightless and free of pressure and exertion. Keep your eyes slightly open and your mouth closed. With closed eyes, one easily falls into a dull and dreamy state. Your gaze should, however, be lowered and not fixed on any particular object. Experience has shown that the mind is quietest and freest of strain or fatigue when the eyes are lowered in this way.

"Your spine should always be straight. This is particularly important. If the body slumps, not only are the internal organs subjected to excessive pressure and prevented from functioning freely, but the vertebrae may also be placed under strain and press on the nerves. Since mind and body are one, anything that harms the body inevitably harms the mind too, endangering the clarity and 'single-pointedness' that are vital to effective concentration. From the standpoint of growing and maturing, a 'ramrod' posture is quite as undesirable as a slovenly one, for the first expresses pride and the second an abject lack of self-discipline. Both are grounded in the puny ego, and are therefore equally obstructive on the path to enlightenment. Always remember to hold your head up; if it is bent forward or to one side and remains in that position for some time, you will be left with a stiff neck."

Maintaining the right posture is essentially a matter of working all the time to keep the correct verticals upright and anchored in the firm horizontals of the stomach-pelvis-diaphragm complex, or *hara*. [17] The most helpful image here is that of the "rooted stick"; with every breath, its roots go deeper into the earth, while its trunk and crown grow upward. But again and again we find that we have slumped a little, letting the abdomen go slack or drawing it in, and depriving the spinal column of the natural supporting power it can have only when it is completely vertical—and that the head has slipped forward or back as a result. And so, again and again we must straighten up—never minding about the hollow back! A position that at first seems unnaturally erect and stiff (the "ramrod") instantly feels right when we follow orders and "push the buttocks back" (as Zen cheerfully puts it, "Let your anus see the sun!"), while pressing the abdomen slightly into the groin. Suddenly we feel the body straightening itself effortlessly, of its own accord—and feel ourselves growing and expanding upward, downward, and in all directions.

Working on Consciousness

The transformation of consciousness sought in Zen practice includes both the content and form of consciousness—in other words, we start by emptying consciousness, and then we transform consciousness itself.

Emptying consciousness. When we are trying to rid ourselves of the persistent images, notions, and thoughts that prevent us from "plumbing the depths," the first rule is to let them pass like clouds on the wind.

In its normal waking state, the ego always has objects of consciousness. One way of getting rid of them is to let the ego focus on an object that eventually swallows it! Breathing, or rather the closely followed rhythm of breathing, is the favorite "object" for this purpose. As this natural "out-out-in" pattern gradually infiltrates our consciousness, we approach the point where true meditation takes over from "concentration," object-centered tension is dissipated, and we are left in

17. Cf. Dürckheim, *Hara: The Vital Centre of Man.*

a rhythmically "tuned" state that entirely fills our consciousness. This tuned state is what matters: the music of Being rings out all the time, and we must become tuned instruments so that it can be heard through us.

Counting breaths is one traditional way of keeping images and thoughts at bay. We are told to count to ten and start again—this is meant to stop us from taking pride in our "score" or becoming drowsy from counting on indefinitely.

If we do not stare at the spot we look at in meditation, but simply let our gaze rest upon it, it too can effect the switch from objective to subjective consciousness. Suddenly it is no longer "outside," but "inside" too, and we and it are one. When this happens, both ego and object cease to exist.

We can also empty consciousness by concentrating on the point where our two thumbs touch, simply registering the sensation at the point where they meet. To eliminate "pressure" on the thumbs at that point, it is best not to place the entire left hand in the palm of the right, but simply to lay the fingers of the left hand on the fingers of the right. When this is done, the thumbs automatically touch very lightly.

Transforming consciousness. To transform consciousness is, first and foremost, to substitute sense consciousness for objective consciousness, and we can do this best by focusing on our own immediate sense impressions. The question here is, what do we really, subjectively sense when we objectively know, for example, that our thumbs are touching each other, our foot is resting, or our buttocks are touching the floor at a certain point? Normally, what we "sense" is immediately turned into what we "know"—but now we are trying to restore the original contact, to feel the quality of what we sense and the quality of our own sensations. We should focus on breathing in this way, not as something happening in a particular place, something we have or do, but as change and movement *which we are.* When we exercise, we must feel ourselves responding to the rhythmic quality of our own movements and must bring out their meaning as something we both experience and are. Any action that becomes automatic can be performed in this way. Indeed, daily life is full of these automatic actions, and the student of Zen learns to use them to make contact with his inner self again and again throughout the day.[18] This is also the secret of the mantra's power to transform. Recited over and over again, either aloud or only to ourselves, it breaks the spell of objective consciousness, opens the door, and allows us to become one with our own inner nature. It is sheer repetition, rather than content, that allows this. Obviously, it only works in the right way if the mind is entirely focused on union with the Absolute.

We can ease the transition from objective to sense consciousness in zazen if we stop thinking of consciousness as being located in the head (forehead) and think of it as being in the back of the neck or the upper part of the spinal column instead, that is, if we sense ourselves at that point and "see" from it. The spot on which our eyes rest in meditation can also be "seen" like this—and what we see then is totally different from what we see with defining, cerebral consciousness. The new consciousness might be said to be neither mental consciousness, which has developed in the cerebrum, nor pre-mental consciousness, which is located in the cerebellum and has a more primal quality, but post-mental consciousness diffused throughout the body—just as total change when we merge with Buddha-nature is also experienced as something affecting the whole body.

The state of consciousness we try to attain on the path to our true nature is not merely supra-objective, but supra-dualistic as well. We can bring it closer by "enduring" feelings, sensations, and even pain (e.g., in the legs), which have intensified to a point where they can scarcely be borne. When unendurable pain is nonetheless endured with complete serenity, a state of being beyond pain and non-pain *may* develop.

18. Cf. Karlfried Graf Dürckheim, *The Way of Transformation: Daily Life as a Spiritual Exercise*, trans. Ruth Lewinnek and P. L. Travers (London: Unwin Paperbacks, 1980).

Breathing

No one can practice zazen meaningfully and helpfully without knowing how to breathe correctly. The zazen approach to breathing shows particularly clearly how far Zen is from the merely artificial and how its way to the truth always leads through the deeply natural or immediate needs of a given situation. "This and this only" is the one rule, and everything that Zen demands of correct posture is summed up in the two words *this only*. This is why Zen breathing is a long way, for example, from hatha yoga breathing. The only change Zen tries to make is to eliminate the distortion of natural breathing that occurs chiefly when the ego predominates and the correct center of gravity is shifted upward, with the result that auxiliary muscles are called in to do the job that should normally be done by the diaphragm.

Bringing into awareness the real meaning of breathing as change and movement, as well as the meaning carried by each of the phases of natural breathing, has been found a useful way of dismantling ingrained bad habits in zazen. Put in the simplest terms, in seeking to achieve union with the Absolute, or whatever name one gives it, one must stop identifying with the objectively defining ego, which clings to its fixed positions.

When functioning properly, natural breathing goes a long way toward doing this job for us. It is a question of opening our eyes to the process and experiencing it consciously, i.e., participating in it consciously while exercising. We can do this very simply by learning to think of breathing not merely as a way of taking in air and expelling it, but as a movement in which we open and close *ourselves,* give *ourselves,* and, thus renewed, receive *ourselves* back again. When he breathes out, the student of zazen must feel that he is freeing himself of everything that has become fixed and static, and making room for the movement of renewal that he can experience when he breathes in. When breathing follows its natural, primal, and healthy rhythm, breathing in normally takes a quarter of the time required for the whole operation. Breathing out and the pause between out and in account for the remaining three-quarters and prepare for the natural expansion of breathing in. In this second phase, we (1) relax, (2) settle, and (3) merge; or, more accurately, (1) relax the upper body (shoulders, chest), which has been drawn up, (2) settle in the pelvic region, or *hara,* and (3) merge with the pelvic base. When we do this properly, breathing in becomes automatic and is experienced as revitalization and renewal of the whole system. One formula, which says it more profoundly and can be used to accompany breathing, runs: give oneself, give oneself over, give oneself up, and (breathing in) receive oneself back again, renewed.

Breathing out is thus the only phase in which we actually "do" anything; breathing in is automatic. Obviously, we only breathe like this—consciously fulfilling the purpose of breathing—during the concentration phase before every exercise. Once breathing becomes automatic, the meditation phase proper begins.

Only someone who has practiced zazen correctly and with the greatest regularity for at least a few months can judge what it has to offer. The traditional minimum exercise period is thirty to forty minutes.

The Three Stages of Consciousness and the Five Steps on the Way

We have seen that our true nature is the mode in which divine Being seeks to manifest itself in us, and that it cannot do this while the objective ego and its values hold sway. To become conscious (i.e., to "enter" awareness) of Being, we need a new consciousness, subjective consciousness, in which Being and consciousness become a single indwelling presence. The purpose of Zen is to liberate subjective consciousness.

We are so totally absorbed by the things we know, can

do, and are used to, that we rarely notice the reflected glow of a new, unknown, and greater life just over the rim of our ordinary consciousness. This ordinary consciousness is like an island and we are like islanders; we can imagine nothing outside our island, and although the sea is all around us, we have no idea what it is or how far it reaches. An inexplicable mystery is woven through our whole existence, but its only links with our ordinary consciousness are subliminal. Like stars in daylight, it is hidden from us by the light of our own objective consciousness, even though our purpose and destiny in life is to let it become manifest in and through ourselves. Every initiation process, every "way" of practice, sets out to make this happen—including Zen.

The way we human beings follow is the way of developing consciousness, and this consists of three stages.[19] We start at the *pre-mental* stage, where we are still "beyond" antitheses, where undivided consciousness expresses undivided life. Our ultimate goal is the higher, *post-mental* stage, which also lies "beyond" antitheses; this is the stage aimed at in Zen. The *mental* stage lies between the two and is governed by the defining ego.

Thus, the word *beyond* has a double meaning that applies to two stages: pre-mental and post-mental. The "beyond" itself is an active principle, sustaining and stimulating us on the deepest level of our consciousness, though we gradually lose touch with it as our intellect develops. And it is something we can find our way back to by outgrowing the consciousness that alienates us from our roots. Zen wisdom focuses on that spiritual level at which our ordinary consciousness is left behind, and Life is experienced post-mentally and not pre-mentally. Obviously, this experience comes more easily if Life is still subliminally active deep within us. If, on the other hand, we can no longer sense its presence, take it seriously, or accept its manifestations as anything but childish or primitive, we will find it hard to make contact with Zen.

19. Jean Gebser, *The Ever-Present Origin* (Athens, Ohio: Ohio University Press, 1985).

We cannot survive unscathed even during the stage when developing objective consciousness has alienated us from our primal, pre-objective consciousness, unless we are still secretly in contact with Being. If objective consciousness and its logic, aesthetics, and ethics sever this contact completely, we eventually reach a point where the only alternative to total stagnation is breaking through to the third, post-mental stage.

The three stages of consciousness can be subdivided into five steps. The transition from pre-mental to mental is the first. The second, third, and fourth are all taken at the mental stage of consciousness, which serves as a springboard to the post-mental stage.

The second step is emergence and development of the objective, dualistic consciousness, which lands us simultaneously in the antitheses of ego/world and ego/true nature. To start with, however, the ego/world tension is the only one we feel. Suppressing true nature and our roots in Being, we concentrate entirely on the world, on succeeding in it, surviving in it, and doing what it asks of us, and the gap separating us from Being widens.

The third step comes when the ego/world tension crushes our true nature, and the resultant anguish drives us in on ourselves. We now try to evade the world's demands, but these demands are unceasing, and we are torn between living for the world and living for our own inner selves. True nature calls from the inner life, and by trying to live that life only, we accentuate the tension between our inner needs and the world's demands. This tension is the central feature of the third step. When the strain increases to breaking point, we are ready to take the fourth.

We take the fourth step only when a first experience of our own true nature—and of the Absolute in our own true nature—has liberated us, filled us with joy, and sent us looking for stability somewhere outside the inner-life/worldly-life antithesis. This means turning our backs on the world and trying repeatedly to sense our true nature in "private" meditation, to dwell in Being beyond the antithesis. Since contact with Being releases us from anguish, we naturally try to prolong it. Of course, this pursuit of unworldly tranquility may be simple escapism, an attempt to live in the past or to reclaim the sheltered world of childhood. But it can also start something new, generate a new sense of purpose, and lead to genuine fulfillment.

All this time, the ego and our links with the world are still inescapably there, and so a day inevitably comes when we realize that the peace we seem to have found outside life's contradictions is actually the peace of indolence. Repressing our true nature was one way of failing to become a complete human being—and we fail again now if we try to pretend that we have no ego, that we are not in the world, and that the contradiction between absolute true nature and contingent reality has simply disappeared. Just when we think we have outrun all of life's contradictions, we run slap into the one contradiction that cannot be removed, that will not go away. And so we are forced again and again to face up to the ego and our human destiny. We must return to the world and accept the pain caused by the tension between relative and absolute. If at this point we forget what the fourth step has taught us and simply regress to the old ego, all may be lost. But if we can genuinely outgrow antitheses by accepting them, we can at last make the breakthrough to post-mental consciousness, which was already close when the fourth step was taken. This is the fifth step, the decisive step into the true self, where ego and true nature become one.

When we take the fifth step, we experience satori and the opening of the inner eye, which sees Being and existence as one. It is only at this point that we can stop seeing dualistic existence and non-dualistic Being as opposites, and start perceiving Being *in* existence. When we take the fourth step, we try to lose the ego in true nature. When we take the fifth step, we must accept the ego all over again. It is only by learning to see antitheses as the form in which the not-two presents itself to us when it passes through the prism of the defining consciousness that we can accept the pain caused us by the conflict of light and darkness, good and evil, Being and non-Being—and make something positive of it. The fact that we are now anchored in true nature, somewhere beyond suffering and non-suffering, does not mean that we stop suffering, but simply that we can now suffer *usefully.* From now on, our pain is no longer the pain that has no purpose, embitters, means nothing, and cannot be escaped; it is the pain that benefits us and makes us over. Now that we have experienced something beyond cause and effect, and have seen through that relationship, we can meet life's reverses in a new way and use our new freedom to turn them around and make them positive. We have reached the ground of all things, and can now accept our destiny—however hard—shape it, and make the most of it in a way that often seems superhuman to the ordinary consciousness. In fact, all of this only shows what human beings *really* are, deep down, when wholeness is achieved. The ways in which we experience the world and respond to it have been transformed. The Absolute lives on "subjectively" within us, and the pain of relativity also acquires a new meaning; for, whatever happens, we are now aware of creative, redemptive Being as an omnipresent force, constantly, lovingly drawing us home to the ground in which all things are one, and also constantly remaking us and releasing us back into the world.

The five-step formula runs through the whole of human life, as long as life keeps on the move and advances dialectically toward fulfillment in the not-two. Our conscious life is tensioned between poles, with first one and then the other "winning," and it ceases to be real in a nonpolar universe where these poles are suspended. We reject the relative when we turn our backs on the world, but it is only by accepting it again and finding the Absolute, which we have now experienced, in the very heart of relativity that we can approach fulfillment.

Zen thinks, lives, and practices the five-step dialectic of life. The dialectic we go through in practice (and going through it is more than merely thinking it) has symbolic force for human life as well, when it is lived, suffered, and shaped "to the end that is fulfillment."

I have my Zen teacher, Takeharu Teramoto, to thank for a text of inexhaustible profundity—"The Tale of the Wonderful Art of a Cat"—which gives a uniquely vivid picture of the five-step dialectic.

Takeharu Teramoto was a former admiral and a professor at the Naval Academy in Tokyo. His practice *(gyo)* was fencing, and the story of the five cats was passed on to him by his fencing master—the last in a school where it had been handed down from master to master since the early seventeenth century as a secret guide to practice.

The Tale of the Wonderful Art of a Cat

There was once a master swordsman named Shoken. His household was plagued by an enormous rat, which ran boldly back and forth even in broad daylight. One day, Shoken put his cat into the room and closed the door behind it, so it could catch the rat; but the rat sprang at the cat and bit it in the face so savagely that it ran off howling—and so this attempt came to nothing. Next, Shoken brought in a number of neighboring cats with good reputations and put them into the room. The rat crouched in a corner and leaped at any cat that came near, biting it and putting it to flight. It looked so ferocious that none of the cats was eager to risk taking it on again. At this stage, Shoken lost his temper and set out to chase and kill the rat himself. But in spite of all his skill, it slipped past his every blow and he could not catch it, although he put his sword through doors, shojis, and karakamis in trying. The rat darted like lightning through the air, dodged his every slash and thrust, sprang at him, and bit him in the face. Finally, sweating and exhausted, he shouted to his servant, "Six or seven leagues from here, there's a cat that's supposed to be the cleverest in the world—go and get it!"

The servant fetched the cat. She looked much the same as the others—neither particularly clever nor particularly fierce—and so Shoken expected nothing special of her. All the same, he opened the door cautiously and let her in. The cat advanced very calmly and slowly into the room, as if she too were expecting nothing out of the ordinary. The rat, however, gave a start and did not stir. The cat simply walked unhurriedly up to it, picked it up in her mouth, and carried it out.

That evening, the defeated cats met in Shoken's house, respectfully offered the old cat the place of honor, bowed down before her, and said humbly, "We are all considered hardworking. We have all practiced our skills and sharpened our claws so that we can win against rats of all kinds, and even weasels and otters. We would never have thought that such a strong rat could exist. How did you manage to beat it so easily? Please do not keep your secret to yourself, but tell us how you did it!"

The old cat laughed and said, "True enough, all you young cats are hardworking, but you do not know the right way, and so you fail when something unexpected comes along. But first tell me how you have practiced."

A black cat stepped forward and said, "I come from a family famous for its rat-catching, and decided to follow the same path myself. I can jump over a screen two meters high. I can force myself through a hole so small that only a rat can get through it. Since I was a kitten, I have practiced all the acrobatic tricks. Even when I'm waking up, still half-asleep and struggling to rouse myself, one glimpse of a rat flitting along a beam—I've got it at once. But that rat today was stronger than I, and I suffered the most terrible defeat of my career. I am deeply ashamed.''

"What you have practiced," said the old cat, "is technique and nothing else [*shosa,* or purely physical skill], but you are constantly asking yourself, 'How can I win?' and so you are always clinging to a goal! When the great masters of the past taught 'technique,' they did it to show their students *one form of the way* [*michisuji*]. Their technique was simple—and yet it contained the loftiest truth. But technique itself is the only thing people care about today. Of course they've come up with plenty of new tricks on the 'such-and-such results from doing so-and-so' principle. But what is the real result? Some new sleight of hand and nothing else. And so the old way has been forgotten and people have worn their brains out trying to outdo one another with better techniques. Now every single possibility has been exhausted and there aren't any stones left to turn. This is what always happens when technique is the only thing that matters and people rely entirely on their cleverness. It's true, of course, that cleverness is a spiritual function, but if it isn't based on the way and aims only at skill, it puts you on the wrong track, and everything you do turns out badly. So look for the truth in yourself and practice properly from now on.''

Next a large tabby cat stepped forward and said, "I believe that mind is the only thing that counts in the martial arts; that is why I have always tried to develop my mental power [*ki wo nero*]. As a result, I feel that my mind is as hard as steel, free, and charged with the 'spirit of *ki*' that fills heaven and earth [Mencius]. The moment I see the foe, this omnipotent spirit casts its spell on him, and I've won before I've even started. Only then do I make my move—very simply, doing only what the situation requires. I can hear my opponent think, I can use my power to steer him left or right as I choose, and I always know what he's going to do before he does it. I never give technique a thought—technique looks after itself. When a rat runs out along a beam, I just give him a piercing look. At once he comes tumbling down and I've got him! But that rat is a mystery; it comes without form and goes without a trace. What's it all about? I don't know."

"It is true," the old cat said, "that what you have sought is the effect that comes from the mighty power that fills heaven and earth. But what you have attained is merely psychic power and is not good in the true sense of the term. The very fact that you are conscious of the power on which you count for victory works against your winning, since your ego is in play. What happens when your opponent's ego is stronger than your own? You hope to crush him with your superior power—and he turns his power on you! Do you really think that you alone are strong and everyone else weak? What are you going to do when you meet something that your own strength, great as it is, is not sufficient to defeat? That is the question! The inner power that you feel and that seems 'free,' 'as hard as steel,' and 'to fill heaven and earth' is not the mighty power [*ki no sho*], but only its reflection in yourself. It is your own mind, and hence only the shadow of the great spirit. Of course, it looks very like this great, all-embracing power, but it's really something totally different. The spirit of which Mencius speaks is strong because it is permanently illuminated by a great clarity—but your mind is strong only under certain conditions. Your mind and the spirit of which Mencius speaks come from different sources, and so have different effects. The difference between them is the difference between an eternally flowing river, like the Yangtse, and an overnight flood. What kind of power do you need when you find yourself face to face with something that contingent spiritual power [*kisei*] can never conquer? Remember the old proverb: 'A cornered rat will even bite the cat.' When your foe is cornered and facing death, nothing can touch him anymore. He forgets life, pain, himself—and no longer gives a straw for victory or defeat. He no longer has any intention of protecting his own safety. That is why his will is as hard as steel. How can you hope to defeat him with spiritual powers for which you take credit yourself?"

An older, gray cat now came slowly forward and said:

"Everything you say is true. Psychic power, however great, always has an inner form [*katachi*], and anything, however small, that has form is tangible. And so for many years I have sought to develop my soul [*kokoro*, the power of the heart]. I do not employ the power that overcomes others from the mind [the *sei* used by the second cat]. Nor do I use claws and teeth [like the first cat]. I make peace with my opponent, allow myself to go along with him, and do absolutely nothing to resist him. If he is stronger, I simply give in and make him feel that I'm doing what he wants. You might say that my art is the art of catching flying stones in a loose curtain. Any rat, however strong, that tries to attack me finds nothing to jump at, nothing to catch hold of. But that rat today simply wouldn't play my game. It came and went as mysteriously as God himself. I've never seen anything like it."

"What you call making peace," said the old cat, "is not rooted in true nature, in the great nature of all things. It is a manufactured, artificial way of making peace—a trick—and you are consciously using it to escape your enemy's aggression. But because you think this—if only for an instant—he sees what you are up to. If you try to seem conciliatory in this frame of mind, you merely confuse and obscure your own aggressive instinct and take the edge off your own perceptions and actions. Anything you do with a conscious intention inhibits the primal, secret impetus of nature and checks its spontaneous flow. How can you expect to work miracles like that? It is only when you think nothing, want nothing, do nothing, and surrender yourself and your own rhythm to the rhythm of true nature [*shizen no ka*] that you shed tangible form—and counter-form becomes impossible. When that happens, there can be no more enemies to resist.

"I do not believe for a moment that all the things you have practiced are useless. Everything—absolutely everything—can be a form of the way. Technique and the way can also be one and the same thing, and the all-governing spirit is then contained in technique and speaks through the body's actions as well. The power of the great spirit [*ki*] serves the human person [*ishi*]. If your *ki* has been liberated, you are endlessly free to respond to everything in the right way. If your spirit is genuinely at peace, neither gold nor stone can harm it, and you need no special skills in battle. Only one thing counts: there must not be a breath of ego-consciousness anywhere, or everything is lost. If you think about it even for a moment, all of this becomes artificial and no longer flows from true nature, from the primal motion of the body of the way [*do-tai*]. When this happens, your enemy, too, will resist instead of doing what you want. And so, what method or art do you need? It is only when you are entirely free of consciousness [*mushin*], when you act without acting, with no intentions or tricks, in harmony with the nature of all things, that you are on the right way. So have no intentions, practice having no intentions—and simply let things happen from true nature. This way is endless and inexhaustible.''

And then the old cat went on to say something astonishing: "You must not imagine that what I have told you here is the last word. Not long ago, there was a tomcat living in the village next to mine. He slept all day, and there wasn't a trace of anything that looked like spiritual power about him; he just lay there like a block of wood. No one had ever seen him catch a rat, but there were no rats when he was around—and wherever he showed up or settled down, there wasn't a rat to be seen! One day I went over to see him and asked him to explain the whole thing. He said nothing—and still said nothing when I repeated my question, and repeated it twice after that. But it wasn't really that he didn't want to answer; he obviously didn't know what to say. And so I saw that those who know do not speak, and those who speak do not know. That cat had forgotten himself and everything around him as well. He had become 'nothing,' he had achieved the highest form of non-volition. You might even say that he'd found the divine way of knighthood—conquering without killing. I'm still a long way short of that myself.''

As if in a dream, Shoken overheard all of this. Coming up, he greeted the old cat and said, "I have practiced the sword for many years now, but have still not reached the goal. Now I have listened to your wise words and feel that I understand the true meaning and purpose of my way—but I implore you to tell me more about your secret."

"How can I do that?" the old cat said. "I am only an animal, and rats are my food. How can I know about human concerns? All I know is that swordplay is not merely a matter of defeating an opponent, but an art that can ultimately lead a person into the great brightness of the radiant ground of death and life [*seishi wo akiraki ni suru*]. Even while he is performing his technical exercises, a true master should constantly perform the spiritual exercise that leads him to this clarity—and to do this he must study the doctrine of the basis of life and death in Being and of the meaning of death [*shi no ri*]. You can attain ultimate clarity only by freeing yourself of everything that leads you astray from this way [*hen kyoku,* the middle distance], and particularly of defining thought. If true nature and contact with true nature [*shin ki*] are interfered with neither by the ego nor by anything else, they are perfectly free to manifest themselves whenever this is necessary. But if your heart clings—even fleetingly—to anything, true nature is imprisoned and turned into something fixed and static. When this happens, there is also a fixed and static ego, and something fixed and static outside that resists it. And so there are now two things standing facing each other and battling for survival—and the wonderful workings of true nature, whose essence is constant change, are impeded. This is the grip of death, and the clarity of true nature has been lost. If you are in this state, how can you meet your enemy in the right frame of mind and look calmly on victory and defeat? Even victory, if it came, would be a blind victory and would have nothing to do with the meaning and purpose of true swordsmanship.

"Being free of all things does not mean a vacuum. True nature as such has no inherent nature of its own, but lies beyond all forms. It takes in nothing from outside, but its vital force sticks to anything, however trivial, to which we cling, however briefly—and the primal balance of energies is lost. If checked even slightly, true nature is no longer free to pour itself out abundantly. When its balance is disturbed, it floods the points it still reaches, and the points it does not reach are starved. In the first case there is too much energy and no way of stopping it. In the second there is too little, and the spirit of action is weakened and fails. In both cases it becomes impossible to do what the actual situation requires. And so, when I speak of being free of all things, all I mean is this: If one hoards nothing, depends on nothing, and defines nothing, there is neither subject nor object, neither ego nor anti-ego. When something comes, one meets it as if unconsciously and it leaves no trace. The *I Ching* says: 'No thought, no action, no movement, total stillness: only thus can one manifest the true nature and law of things from within and unconsciously, and at last become one with heaven and earth.' Anyone who practices and understands swordsmanship in this manner is close to the truth of the way.''

When he heard this, Shoken asked, "What do you mean when you say there is neither an ego nor an anti-ego, neither a subject nor an object?''

The cat replied: "When there is an ego—and because there is an ego—there is also an enemy. If we do not set ourselves up as egos, there is no one and nothing to oppose us. When we speak of an opponent or enemy, we really mean an opposing principle. Whenever a thing has form, it also has an anti-form—and it has form as soon as it becomes definite. If my true nature has no form, then no anti-form exists. Without an antithesis, there is no opposing principle, and this means that there is neither an ego nor an anti-ego. If we let ourselves go completely and become entirely, fundamentally detached, we are in harmony with the world, at one with all things in the great All-One. Even when our enemy's form is extinguished, we are completely unconscious of this, in the sense that we do not dwell on it. Our mind moves freely on without defining anything, and our actions flow straight from our true nature.

"When our spirit is entirely free and unoccupied, then

we and the world are entirely one. This means that we now accept it beyond good and evil, beyond liking and disliking. Nothing holds us back and we no longer cling to anything. All the antitheses we encounter—profit and loss, good and evil, joy and suffering—come from ourselves. That is why there is nothing in heaven or on earth more worth the knowing than our own true nature. An ancient poet says: 'A speck of dust in your eye and three worlds are too narrow; care for nothing and the straitest bed is broad enough.' In other words, if a speck of dust penetrates the eye, the eye cannot open, for it can see only when there is nothing in it. This can serve as a metaphor for Being—the light that shines and illuminates, in which there is nothing that is 'something,' but which loses its virtue the moment 'something' enters it. Another poet says: 'If I am surrounded on all sides by enemies, one hundred thousand in number, my form is crushed into nothingness. But my true nature is eternally mine, however strong the foe may be. No enemy can ever penetrate it.' Confucius says: 'Even a simple man's true nature cannot be stolen from him.' If our spirit becomes confused, our own true nature turns against us.

"That is all I can tell you. Simply look for the truth within yourself. All a master can do is tell his student the basics and try to explain them. But only you yourself can find out the truth and make it your own. This is called self-appropriation [*jitoku*]. The message is transmitted from heart to heart [*i shin den shin*] in a special way that lies beyond formal instruction and scholarship [*kyogai betsuden*]. This does not mean that what the masters taught was wrong, but simply that even a master cannot pass on the truth. This is not true of Zen only. In the spiritual exercises of the ancients, in cultivation of the soul and in the fine arts, self-appropriation has always been the vital element—and this is transmitted only from heart to heart, beyond all tradition and instruction. The purpose of 'instruction' is always merely to point the way to something all of us already have without knowing it. And so there is no 'mystery' that a master can 'pass on' to his student. To instruct is easy. To listen is easy. But it is hard to become aware of what one has within oneself, to track it down and take possession of it properly. This is what we call looking into our own true nature [*ken-sei, ken-sho*]. When we do this, we experience satori, the great awakening from the dream of error and illusion. To wake, to look into one's nature, to perceive the truth of oneself—all of these are the same thing."

Zen for the West — Western Zen

In its essence, there can be no doubt that Zen, as taught in the East, is not merely Oriental, but holds the answer to one of the vital needs of people in the West as well. Only people who cannot see what Zen is really about are put off by its specifically Eastern trappings.

We must remember, however, that Easterners and Westerners do see the purpose of human life differently—and we must face up to the differences if Zen's basic insights, teachings, and exercises are to help us. The fundamental difference is between the ways in which East and West see the coming of Life to *form*.

Human beings are ruled by two conflicting instincts, the urge to escape the world and the urge to shape it. There is a permanent difference between East and West regarding the relationship between the two, and each runs the danger of seeing one side only. The danger in the East is that of simply letting go and dissolving in the Absolute, while the danger in the West is that of letting fixed forms choke the vital impulse, of seeing life only as a series of fragmented details. Both East and West can learn important lessons from the dangers that threaten them.

In both East and West, to be genuinely enlightened is to see both sides—and to see that they are indivisibly connected—whether or not one's own tradition stresses one side at the other's expense. Even when it counts as the more important of the two, "seeing the whole" makes sense only as a prelude to "seeing the parts," and seeing the parts makes sense only when it comes of repeatedly seeing the whole. Contraction and expansion *together* make up the natural rhythm of breathing and growth. And yet there is a difference of emphasis between East and West: the East emphasizes union with the Absolute and ultimate extinction of the ego (and even the individual soul) in Being, while the West emphasizes the coming of the Absolute to form in the here-and-now. For us Westerners, this question of form is central, and our nature and traditions are such that giving the Absolute a form is our special responsibility.

The purpose of trying to do anything well in Zen is to achieve union with the Absolute. Even when the immediate aim in performing an exercise is to perfect a skill, that exercise is really concerned with what is going on inside as a person sees where his ways of acting and thinking are wrong, discards his bad habits, and moves from tentative contact to a genuine, deepening awareness of Being in his true nature. The only value of what he does or produces "along the way" lies in the degree to which it reflects his contact with Being. In the West, however, we are the heirs of the Platonic tradition; we think that form has inherent meaning and value, and try to perfect it for its own sake. We feel a duty not only to human development, but to formal perfection as well. Life's meaning, as promised by our share in Being, is not simply redemption; it is also the "work" that bears witness to Being.

This is true of everything people make, and even truer of people themselves. We see human perfection in the human *person,* expressing Life in a valid form (in Christian terms, the Word becoming flesh).

This belief that all creatures—and human beings too—fulfill themselves in a physical, specific, and perfected form lies at the heart of the Western intellectual tradition. An essential part of that tradition is the conviction that Being must take on form in persons—an assumption that the East, with another outlook and tradition, does not share. Indeed, it is significant that the Japanese had no words for *personality* or *work* (in the sense of a specific thing made by a specific person) until very recently.

The three essential facets of Being—fullness, order, and unity—are revealed as clearly to people in the East as they are to us. In Eastern deities, as in our own, they are reflected in the attributes of power, wisdom, and love. In Buddhism itself, they appear as the threefold treasure: Buddha, the doctrine, and the community of disciples.

Of course, in both East and West, the threefold unity of Being is also reflected in the view that people naturally take of one another. Like the Westerner, the Easterner is drawn to, loves, and respects the person who expresses the fullness and unity of Being in his energy and capacity for loving, but who also has firm outlines that neither energy nor love can blur. Eastern art, like that of the West, has an unmistakable feeling for form, perfect form to which nothing can be added, and from which nothing can be taken away. But form has a different significance in the East.

When we in the West take aesthetic pleasure in an artifact—a picture or statue, for instance—our pleasure comes from what we see. But the Easterner looks beyond what he sees to the underlying reality, from which all forms come and to which they return, but which is itself beyond both form and formlessness. For him, a flower in full bloom is only one of the countless ways in which the Absolute manifests itself—a specific reflection of it. For us, the form in which Being reveals itself is itself the point, and formal perfection completes and consummates a process. This is the process of becoming, and we see its ultimate goal not as release from a multiplicity of forms into the One, but as revelation of the One in form (absolute in contingent form). At the second stage of consciousness, the impulse from Being that makes us seek perfection becomes trapped and distorted in fixed forms, and the primal experience is rationalized, rigidified, cut off from Being, and ultimately stifled—but this is only an aberrant form of what is really meant. The East calls this condition "the Western sickness of form," and we are now becoming aware of it ourselves, and starting to rebel against the merely formal and fixed. Zen and Zen exercise can help us to make this rebellion fruitful. This is why artists and psychologists are turning to Zen, and why people who have lost their beliefs are increasingly using zazen-type meditation to empty themselves and prepare for the primal experience of Being. This experience underlies all live religious feeling, but once-for-all interpretation of it leads to pseudo-belief and lip service, and turns practice into dead formalism.

Once, only intellectuals and artists saw the truth about form. Now a whole generation is dimly starting to realize that forms—the forms we make and the forms we are—are alive only when Being shines through them. The East can teach us a lot about making this happen. Zen meditation sets out to remake us, turning us into mediums for Being, and its insistence on correct posture means that the message is, as it were, written into our bodies as well. This emphasis on "person" as "form" and "form" as "person" introduces a new element, making it necessary to take Zen practice further and bring it closer to Western and traditional Christian conceptions of both person and form. What is needed here is a Western Zen.

The threefold unity of Being is active in every living creature, and every living creature bears the mark of its fullness, essential form, and unity, sustaining us, shaping us, and bringing us to wholeness within the Whole. But its essential form (logos, the word) is clearer to us in the West, and this is why giving it external form—in what we do, make, or are—is our special task. For us, an artifact is perfect when the "idea" behind it is fully expressed in its form—and for us the "person" is the idea behind the human form.

The underlying law, "idea," or life principle of our true nature comes to us as an image in our consciousness, and hovers before us as a form that it is our task to realize. Basically, however, Being within us is not so much an innate image as an innate way—the inner way along which the Absolute takes form as we follow it step by step. When we set out consciously upon this way, we experience satori, and our eyes are opened to the signatures and signs that the Absolute uses to reveal its laws, order, and essence, and to manifest itself in individual human beings.

One of the signs that tells a master that his student has awakened and is an entirely new person comes when that student is no longer afraid to be himself. Because he has tasted Being and is now free to become uniquely and utterly himself, he can behave naturally even in front of the master. But here the emphases differ between East and West: the Oriental master sees individuation only as a sign that contact with Being has freed his student of the ego, while we feel that the change that has made him entirely himself was what the experience was really about. For us, the purpose of awakening is to bring out a human being's individuality and to make him fully a person for the first time; we believe he is not a person simply because Being is in him, but because it manifests itself in his particular shape. For us, as for the Oriental, a human being is perfect when Being shines through him and is radiantly reflected in whatever he experiences, is, and does, but we take this perfection above all as meaning that Being has come to valid form in him, is personified in him, and is perfecting others through him.

Even Eastern Zen knows that Being can be experienced only in the form it assumes in the individual's true nature, and that to experience individuality properly is to experience Being as well. If we assume that Zen rejects form, we are on the wrong track, for Zen sees Being not as transcending forms, but as transcending antitheses, i.e., as transcending form and non-form and therefore present in every form as well.

And so there is also room in Zen for form—and for the human person seen as form. This is why a Western Christian will get a gently knowing smile if he tells a Zen master that God is a person and not the impersonal All-One. Of course, the more he insists on the personal element, the more he lays himself open to the suspicion of clinging to that "God" of whom Meister Eckhart said, "When the ego passes out of being, God also passes out of being." Zen denies only one conception of God—the conception that corresponds to the defining ego. I once asked the abbot of the Zen monastery at Sendai, Master Miura, who had read my book on Meister Eckhart, what he thought of the links between Eckhart and Zen. At first he looked at me and said nothing. Then he shot his right hand out like a sword and looked for a moment at the tiny gap between thumb and index before saying: "It's like that. There's barely the thickness of a leaf between them. Better not to touch it!" What did he mean by "the thickness of a leaf"—and why did he say not to touch it? What he was really saying was this: "How can we be sure that Eckhart's Godhead does not include the great Unity, lying beyond person and non-person, of which we speak? And how can you really be sure that the Absolute does not reveal itself to us, too, in a personal form—while we avoid giving it a name for fear that this will merely tie it down in a concept of God rooted in the ego's fears and hopes?" And yet—there is a difference! Even when he has experienced Being as something that cannot be grasped or defined, perhaps the Christian—and not only the Western Christian—*must* still venerate the mystery as "supreme form" and give it the holy name without hesitating. The East, however, shies away from doing this, and surrounds the Absolute with silence.

The West has an instinctive respect for form itself, and thus for the energy contained in form as well, But we, too, are expected to transform ourselves and liberate within ourselves the energies that create form as we advance on our way—and the teachings and practice of Zen can play an important part here. In fact, Zen wisdom—and Zen practice—can be of the greatest help in releasing human creative energies. There is surely nothing more inimical to creativity than the defining ego and the images and concepts in which it moves or fails to move, and which Zen sets out to eradicate. And surely nothing releases a person's creativity more effectively than breaking away from the concepts that imprison him, plunging into the void, and letting the Absolute take over.

People often ask: What is the use of telling us about ways and methods that seem to depend on masters—since we have no masters? The point to remember here is that some of the things a master in the East has to do to prepare his students for satori are already done when a Westerner starts on the quest. Acceptance of the ego, self-assertion, self-reliance, and the disasters repeatedly brought on him by his own conceptual, technical, and organizational skills—these are the things that prepare the average Westerner for something else and eventually bring him to the crossing point without his being aware of it. When we really come to that point and hear—even once, but unmistakably—the voice from "beyond," then we can also hear the master in ourselves, the voice that speaks to us in all of life's crises, telling us to change course and set out upon the way. Today we can already sense the endless vistas that open up within us when the structures in which we have immured ourselves collapse. And this is a sure sign that we are almost ready to start looking for the way to freedom. The moment we become aware of ourselves as the prisoners of fixed concepts and systems, we are ready for this way, where we see our own suffering for what it is, treat our innermost experience as insight, accept the discipline of everyday life as our practice, and at last become willing to take help where we can find it. Help and helpers are nearer today than we imagine—if we will only let them help us.

The vital thing is to realize that Being—as fullness, logos, and all-embracing unity—is entering the inner heart of humanity, and that humanity itself has matured and is ready to receive it. There are millions, not merely thousands, of people who have looked death and ultimate terror in the face, and experienced in this last extremity something that death cannot touch. There are millions of people who have been brought close to madness by despair at their own inability to understand, and who have suddenly sensed something that mere understanding cannot grasp. There are millions who know what it is to be totally alone, and who have found comfort and shelter in the all-embracing One. This is how Being comes to our rescue in life's darkest moments. Everything depends on taking it seriously and seeing it for what it is: inner strength that the everyday world cannot touch, fundamental meaning beyond all understanding, and love whose power is limitless.

To experience Being's saving power is one thing, but there are millions who have also sensed within themselves the ability and duty to shape their lives in a manner consonant with it—feeling for the first time the impetus and promise that drive people to follow Life's law, which is written into the world and which the world must obey. Rounded personality, formal perfection, system and order—these are always the aims of people who cannot see further than the natural ego. But as ultimate aims, they belong to the era that is drawing to a close. They are being replaced by other aims in which the essential core of what the world-ego is and does fulfills its real purpose by becoming a window for Being.

Each of us has focused thus far on being a "personality"—self-reliant, productive, and consciously dedicating our energies and virtues to objective ideals and objective social values. But the time has come to move on and concentrate on becoming a real person, permanently open and faithful to the way, taking on form and accepting it in others only when it allows Being to show through, when it leaves room for further change.

A new generation is growing up today, a generation that has experienced Being for itself, has maintained contact with it, obeys its laws, is wary of its own weaknesses, rejects hypocrisy, and is dedicated to the service of a new world. As the old supremacies lose their power and the old taboos their magic, the old illusory ideals are being rejected and the sober truth of Being is coming into view.

The darker the clouds on our horizon, the readier we are to welcome the light that scatters them utterly. Do we look to the clouds or the light? That is the everlasting, all-dividing question, the fateful question that faces us today. We shall determine who wins out: the old generation that has lost touch with Being, cannot change its ways, and is hurtling to destruction; or the new generation that has developed and matured to become a vessel and medium for Being, and is advancing steadily toward new life—and taking the world with it.